American University Studies

Series I
Germanic Languages and Literature

Vol. 29

PETER LANG
New York · Berne · Frankfurt am Main

Susan E. Cernyak-Spatz

German Holocaust Literature

PETER LANG
New York · Berne · Frankfurt am Main

Library of Congress Cataloging in Publication Data

Cernyak-Spatz, Susan E.,
German Holocaust Literature.

(American University Series. Series I, Germanic
Languages and Literature; vol. 29)
Bibliography: p.
1. German literature – 20th century – History and
criticism.   2. Holocaust, Jewish (1939–1945), in
literature.   3. National socialism in literature.
I. Title.   II. Series.
PT405.C38   1985   830'.9'358   83-49045
ISBN 0-8204-0072-6
ISSN 0721-1392

CIP-Kurztitelaufnahme der Deutschen Bibliothek

Cernyak-Spatz, Susan E.:
German Holocaust Literature / Susan E. Cernyak-Spatz. –
New York; Berne; Frankfurt am Main: Lang, 1985.
(American University Studies: Ser. 1, Germanic
Languages and Literature; Vol. 29)
ISBN 0-8204-0072-6

NE: American University Studies / 01

© Peter Lang Publishing, Inc., New York 1985

All rights reserved.
Reprint or reproduction, even partially, in all forms such as
microfilm, xerography, microfiche, microcard, offset strictly prohibited.

Printed by Lang Druck, Inc., Liebefeld/Berne (Switzerland)

ACKNOWLEDGMENT

The writer takes this opportunity to express her appreciation to Professor Jadwiga Maurer who initially gave the impetus and encouragement to this study, and to Professor Ruth Angress, whose guidance and interest in this dissertation have been a great help and source of inspiration.

CONTENTS

Introduction		9
Chapter I:	The Political Concentration Camp in the Novel	13
Chapter II:	The Extermination Camp in Novels and Short Stories	47
Chapter III:	The Extermination Camp in the Drama	75
Chapter IV:	Post-War German Literature about the Period Prior to the Holocaust and After the Holocaust	109
List of Works, Secondary Sources and Documentaries		137

INTRODUCTION

The literary works dealing in part or entirely with the events before, during and after the Holocaust could, for the sake of simplification, be considered part of the mid-twentieth century or post-World War II literature. But the events treated in these works are more than just part of the twentieth century. They represent an aberration in the history of civilization that needs to be recorded as a separate entity. Therefore the literature dealing with the concentration camps, German as well as non-German, has become known under the specific sub-heading: Holocaust literature.

The origins of this term have been traced by Gert Korman in a paper given before the American Historical Society in December 1971. He states: "I have used 'Holocaust' in these remarks, but in 1949, there was no 'Holocaust' in the English language in the sense that the word is used today." (1) Korman explains that until 1953 writers spoke about annihilation and destruction in terms of "recent catastrophe," or "the disaster." All these terms, by intent or accident, translated accurately the Hebrew words "shoa" and "hurban." Two years later Yad Vashem (Martyrs and Heroes Remembrance Authority in Israel) translated "shoa" into "disaster." The word "Holocaust" appeared only now and then in connection with the word "disaster." Between 1957 and 1959 the word "Holocaust" was used at the Second World Congress of Jewish Studies held in Jerusalem, and when Yad Vashem published its third yearbook, one of the articles dealt with "Problems relating to a Questionnaire on the Holocaust." Conversion of "the Destruction of

---
(1) Gert Korman, *The Holocaust in American Historiography* from a manuscript graciously lent to the writer by Prof. Korman, p. 10.

European Jewry" into "Holocaust" began before the publication of Raul Hilberg's book *The destruction of the European Jewry* (Quadrangle Books, Inc. 1961). Within the Jewish world the word became commonplace, in part because Elie Wiesel and other gifted writers and speakers made it the coin of the realm. According to Korman, "By 1968, as Jewish scholars in various parts of the world and in various languages revealed, with Jewish sources, the details of the suffering of the Jewish people, the international literature using 'Holocaust' became so significant that the Library of Congress Catalogue Division, committed to a policy of following usage, created a major entry card: 'Holocaust - Jewish, 1939-1945' "(2)

In the words of Gert Korman: "Thus it was that a word brought into the English language by Christian writers centuries ago ... came to be the noun symbolizing ... the destruction of European Jewry." (3)

This study intends to pursue and analyse the development of "Holocaust" literature created by German and German-Jewish authors up to 1970. For this purpose I have chosen representative examples of fictional "Holocaust" literature and drama. I have felt it necessary to include several well-known non-German authors of "Holocaust" fiction, since their treatment of the same events and locations throws additional light on the possibilities of literary evaluation of the subject.

The individual chapters treat the works dealing with the political concentration camp, the extermination camp, the period immediately preceeding the "Holocaust" and the period immediately following the end of the war, as it concerned victims and executioners alike. A definite de-

---

(2) Korman, p. 13.
(3) Korman, p. 15.

velopmental line can be seen in the characterization and point-of-view within the more than twenty year span selected for analysis. The most obvious change becomes apparent in the treatment of the National Socialist German and specifically in the figure of the SS-man. From being the one-dimensional visual representation of an evil system these figures progress to being individual personages whose acts have psychological motivations, regardless whether these motivations were perversion, fanaticism, greed or merely petty-bourgeois zeal. The same kind of individualization can be seen in the characterization of the victims. They too change from pure, noble, defenseless martyrs into three-dimensional persons. Some of them become less good, less pure, less high-minded. In short, they become human beings with strong individual traits, not just "Jewish victims". The most significant development lies in the gradual assumption of responsibility for the events by the whole nation. The writers of the forties and fifties helped their readers to dissociate from the period and its exponents with one-dimensional stereotypes of evil. In the forties German writers depicted generally two distinctly different types of Germans: the good ones, ignorant and innocent of the events, and the comparatively small section of the evil National Socialist Germans who were guilty of all atrocities. By the sixties these attitudes had been left behind and an objective evaluation of a German nation-wide complicity in the "Holocaust" through tacit consent had begun in literary circles. The literary and humanistic development of German literature vis-à-vis this topic within the relatively short span of twenty-five years merits the attention of literary historians.

The selections in this study have been made with a view to the quality of the works. The works chosen are those that may be expected to mirror the moral and intellectual attitudes of their time. This criterion has also been the guideline in the choice of the non-German authors here included.

This study attempts to assess a section of German literature not only as part of the belles-lettres of the twentieth century but also as an overall view of a historical period that has only been evaluated by historians and social scientists.

Instead of adding here some observations about my personal viewpoint and experiences of the "Holocaust" I would like to quote Salo W. Baron, in a foreword to one of Yad Vashem's bibliographies, who has expressed the position of myself and those like me to this topic: " ... a generation that has gone through that extraordinary traumatic experience cannot completely divorce itself from its own painful recollections and look upon the Holocaust from an Archimedian standpoint."(4) The words "concentration camp" and "National Socialism-or Socialist" will be abbreviated throughout to "KZ" and "NS."

---

(4) Lucy S. Davidowicz, "Toward a History of the Holocaust." In *Commentary*, 52, April 1969, 51-56.

CHAPTER I

THE POLITICAL CONCENTRATION CAMP IN THE NOVEL

The Concentration Camp and the Extermination Camp were the two most barbaric features of the Third Reich. The KZ purported to reeducate political dissenters. The Extermination Camp served to eliminate racially undesirable minorities. Many eyewitness accounts and autobiographies have been written about these two institutions, but as a literary subject the many psychological and sociological aspects of camp life have only been exploited to a minor degree by German writers. What developments led to the camps and how, even after the war, they overshadowed the lives of the survivors, the victims as well as the perpetrators, is well documented and available for literary purposes. In spite of these available documents it took more than a decade, until German writers were able to develop objective viewpoints toward the events. The writers of the immediate post-war period, with very few exceptions, seemed to have a need for stereotyping both perpetrators and victims.

German post-war literary treatment of this topic recalls the exile literature treatment of the same subject. Most of the exile writing on the topic had dealt in strong stereotypes to underscore the horrible fate of the victims. This was probably necessary to counteract the waves of professional propaganda emanating from Hitler's Germany. Some writers endeavored to point out that the actions of the regime were not the acts of all Germans, or at least were not committed with the approval of all of them.

Anna Seghers, exiled in Mexico, wrote in this vein. The mixture of nostalgic coloring and one-dimensional stereo-

typing in her novel *Das siebte Kreuz*,(1) a story of the concentration camp, makes this exile work a good example. First published in 1942 in Mexico it clearly shows the manner of stereotyping of NS operatives and their victims that was used in the immediate post-war period by German writers.

According to Seghers' own words, her main aim in creating *Das siebte Kreuz* was to show: "... wie man an einem Ereignis das Verhalten vieler Schichten eines ganzen Volkes zeigen kann."(2) The attitudes of the people depicted by her correspond more to her desire for perpetuating a memory than to the reality of NS Germany of 1934. The reader becomes quickly aware that Seghers believed in the existence of a strong undercurrent of resentment and socialist fervor in the German population of 1934. For this reason there is a feeling of unreality about the work. Seghers took the realistic landscape of the Rhine region and peopled it with characters whose actions are unrealistic for the time-period, however humane and idealistic they might be.

Her detailed knowledge of the landscape can be ascribed to the fact that she was born in that particular region at the turn of the century. Her socialist affiliation prompted her immediate exile in 1933. At that time political dissenters, especially avowed communists, were the main target of NS persecution; the plans for the Jewish persecution were still in preparation. A sense of homesickness, expressed in the loving descriptions of the region, pervades the book.

The story tells of the successful escape of one concentra -

---

(1) Anna Seghers, *Das siebte Kreuz* (Amsterdam: Querido Verlag, V., 1946).
(2) Anna Seghers, "Bewahrung und Entdeckung," in *Neue Deutsche Literatur* XI, 8, (1963), 55.

tion camp prisoner made possible by the cooperation of a large number of his former socialist comrades. Seven men have escaped from KZ Westhofen. Determined to make an example, camp commander Fahrenberg in a barbaric demonstration of his power, has seven wooden crosses erected at the side of Barracks III, where he plans to execute the escapees when they are caught; not *if* but *when* they are caught, since in his mind their capture is a foregone conclusion. Five men are captured and executed after torture and interrogation. One has the good fortune of dying a natural death while he is free. The seventh prisoner, Georg Heisler, manages to flee across the border. His tortuous road to freedom with the help of the many persons, who are spiritually ennobled by their action, forms the main content of the novel. All who help him, expose themselves to grave dangers, but they feel a sense of purpose and solidarity, seemingly forgotten under the pressures of the NS regime.

Georg Heisler's escape becomes a point of obsession for his friends and his enemies. For his friends and comrades it means a symbol of renewed engagement and solidarity with the socialist cause; for his enemy, the regime, it constitutes a warning that prison and torture may not be able to extinguish the spirit of insurrection against injustice. The power of the system seems no longer infallible. Unfortunately, Seghers had overestimated the strength of the socialist forces, since not until 1944 was there any sign of German resistance to the regime and that one was "... actually an ultranationalist response to the possibility of Hitler's losing ..."(3) in the open rebellion of July, 1944.

Paul Rilla points out that the novel is the story of the escape of one concentration camp prisoner: " ... der in den

---
(3) Alexander Donat, "Jewish Resistance," in *Out of the Whirlwind a Reader of Holocaust Literature,* ed. Albert H. Friedlander (Garden City, N.Y.: Doubleday & Co.), 1968, p. 57.

Dörfern am Rhein und Main die Stationen der proletarischen Solidarität durchwandert."(4) Seghers offers the reader a panoramic view of the region surrounding the KZ Westhofen in the Rhine area. The countryside, a living reminder of the history of civilization, is to her a promise of continuity in spite of the aberrations of the time: "Diese Hügel entlang zogen die Römer den Limes. So viele Geschlechter waren verblutet seitdem sie die Sonnenaltäre der Kelten hier ... verbrannt hatten ... Aber nicht den Adler und nicht das Kreuz hat die Stadt dort unten im Wappen behalten, sondern das keltische Sonnenrad...."(5)

Rilla, in the same study also calls this work the novel of a German landscape: " ... untrüglich stand der Dichterin vor Augen was sie schrieb ... die Untrüglichkeit von der auch der Zeitroman seine Wahrheit hatte ... Die Landschaft war kein Naturidyll sondern Menschenstätte. *Das siebte Kreuz* zerstört die Lüge des Idylls ... die Lüge der neuen Heimatliteratur, die idyllische Lüge, die verdecken sollte, was wirklich geschah."(6)

Seghers' knowledge of "her" people is as much colored by her political beliefs as by her nostalgia. She has divided the many personages crowding the pages of her book into good Germans, bad Germans (some of which are still on the borderline between good and evil) and those who consider themselves uninvolved by acting neither for nor against the regime. This last group she sees as guilty by omission.

The good Germans are former, or still secretly active, socialists who only seem to wait for the appearance of a comrade in need of help to take up the severed party con-

---
(4) Paul Rilla, *Die Erzählerin Anna Seghers* (Berlin: Schriftenreihe der deutschen Akademie der Künste, 1950), p. 25.
(5) Anna Seghers, Das Siebte Kreuz, p. 13.
(6) Paul Rilla, p. 26.

nections. In spite of extreme caution and secrecy they seem to have an instinctive knowledge about who is one of them. Among them is Franz Marnet who had been with Georg Heisler: "gemeinsam demonstrieren und auf Versammlungen ..."(7) and Hermann the railroadman, who tells Franz, while talking about the escape: "Jedenfalls müsse man alles bereithalten. Möglich ... dass jemand auftaucht, der Hilfe braucht.... "(8) There is Paul Röder, Heisler's childhood friend, who instinctively turns for help to Fiedler who is also a socialist comrade, though Röder does not know that. Fiedler says of himself: " ... ich gehöre auch noch immer dazu, denn der Paul hat mich ja herausgefunden. Ich finde auch meine Leute wieder."(9) Finally there is Reinhardt, the comrade who provides the final link between Marnet-Hermann, and Röder–Fiedler. Together they arrange for the necessary hiding places, documents and finances for Heisler's escape. Of this human lifeline Rilla says: "Die Rettung des Einen ist die Umsetzung des Anstosses in jene Aktion, die nicht von heute und gestern ist, sondern von lange her vorbereitet war in der Solidarität des proletarischen Kampfes. Die Taktik der Rettung ist die Taktik des illegalen Kampfes ..."(10)

Seghers' description of the bad Germans, i.e. the ones in uniform in the service of the regime, is a stereotyped composite of the traits which Wolfgang Langhoff in his book *Die Moorsoldaten*(11) ascribes to the various personnel of the KZ Börgermoor. Commandant Fahrenberg and Lieutenant Bunsen of Westerhof are described as students *manqués* who had found an opportunity to be big men at the cost of other men's lives: " ... in den Arbeitervierteln herumknallen, Juden verprügeln und dann auf Urlaub nach

---

(7) Anna Seghers, p. 69.
(8) Anna Seghers, p. 64.
(9) Anna Seghers, p. 335.
(10) Paul Rilla, p. 32.
(11) Wolfgang Langhoff, *Die Moorsoldaten: 13 monate*

Hause ... mit Geld in der Tasche, mit Anhang, mit Macht."(12) SA-man Zillich is the type of "dumb brute" who gets promoted in his job because of his aptitude for brutality. To the small group of in-between characters Seghers pays particular attention in spite of their minor roles. To this group belong the active Nazis like the Gestapo commissioner Oberkamp, the Hitler youth Hellwig and Georg Heisler's brother, also an SA-man. Seghers seeks to put redeeming qualities into these characters despite their active collaboration with the regime. All these men seem to have unguarded moments in which questions arise that are salutary to their humanity but harmful to their competence as party members. Oberkamp, for instance: " ... war gewöhnt, in seinem Beruf die Methoden anzuwenden, die polizeiüblich sind ... Auch noch heute hielt er die Menschen, nach denen er fahndete, für die Feinde der Ordnung, wie er sich die Ordnung vorstellte. Somit war alles klar. Unklar wurden die Dinge erst, wenn er sich überlegte, für wen er arbeitete."(13) Young Helwig too has second thoughts in connection with the KZ which are dangerous for his peace of mind: "Lauter Lumpen und Narren waren da sicher nicht drin, sagten die Leute ... Es war ihm ein wenig bang ums Herz ... an diesem Abend war alles abgebrochen für zwei Minuten, Musik und Trommeln, dass man die feinen dünnen Töne hörte, die sonst unhörbar waren."(14) Seghers depicts the main NS figures as one-dimensional negative stereotypes for one reason. For her, as for most exile writers, they represent the outward symbol, the visible part of the evil regime. They are not the human beings who swung the executioner's ax, they *are* the ax, the murder tool. A murder tool has only one

---
    konzentrationslager. Unpolitischer tatsachenbericht (Zurich: Schweizer Spiegel, 1935), p. 158ff.
(12) Anna Seghers, p. 216.
(13) Anna Seghers, p. 298.
(14) Anna Seghers, p. 89.

characteristic: it is evil. This oversimplification, which was logical for the quasi-counterpropagandistic literature of the German exile writers, apparently became the convenient technique for the German Holocaust literature of the forties. The German writers of that period used this oversimplification for the purpose of dissociation.

The group of Germans designated as "guilty by omission" is represented by two academicians: the architect Sauer and the chemist Dr. Kress. Both are aware of the denial of their responsibilities by showing their disapproval of the regime merely through strict non-involvement. Sauer refuses to become active against the regime and pacifies his conscience with the belief that he is thereby protecting his family. Dr. Kress, a former socialist sympathizer, on the other hand, for the sake of regaining the respect of his family, becomes involved by aiding Heisler's escape. Perhaps Seghers is implicitly pointing the finger at a condition which has been elaborated in Bruno Werner's *Die Galeere*.(15) In this work Werner deals with the guilt of the intellectual who stays detached, because he is too sophisticated to accept the Nazi propaganda, but also too unpatriotic and cautious to do more than repeat clever political jokes as a token rejection of the regime.

The peasant families of the region, occupied with their daily chores and with little concern for the political events, seem to be a part of the unchanging scenery before which the frightening events take place. Perhaps Seghers saw a promise of the return to saner times in the unchanging continuity of the country and the tillers of its soil, as it had happened many times throughout history. But she admits that this time history might not repeat itself. This time the country is faced with an indoctrinating apparatus that seems to poison the younger generation and

---

(15) Bruno Werner, *Die Galeere* (Frankfurt a/M: G.B, Fischer Verlag, 1958).

thereby could imperil the historical process: " ... junge Leute, die immer alles besser wissen wollen-nur dass die Jungen in früheren Zeiten das Gute besser wissen wollten, jetzt aber wussten sie das Böse besser."(16)

Seghers uses an innovative structural point throughout the story. The actions and thought of the many individuals cooperating with and involved in the escape plot are narrated simultaneously by an omniscient narrator. But interspersed throughout the story, as well as opening and closing it, we find another narrator: the nameless and faceless KZ inmate who speaks in the first person plural for all the inmates. He narrates only what is seen and heard by the KZ inmates directly. The conjectures, hopes and fears for their escaped comrades, the despair at the capture of five of them, the elation about the success of at least one escape, are all revealed through this camera-eye narration. Through the mouth of the KZ narrator Seghers terms the persecution and extermination of a generation of dedicated socialists the worst evil perpetrated by the NS regime: "Gleich im ersten Monat der Hitlerherrschaft hat man Hunderte unserer Führer ermordet ... Die ganze Generation hat man ausgerottet ... das Furchtbarste, was einem Volk überhaupt geschehen kann, das sollte jetzt uns geschehen: Ein Niemandsland sollte gelegt werden zwischen die Generationen, durch das die alten Erfahrungen nicht mehr dringen konnten.... Da riss man das Beste aus, was im Lande wuchs, weil man die Kinder gelehrt hatte, das sei Unkraut."(17) This work was created in 1942 or shortly before. Viewed from that point in time the concern for the extermination of only one political group distorts the picture. The persecution of the Jews leading to the *Endlösung* (final solution) was in 1934, the time of the narrative, already an openly advocated policy. Seghers' political leanings minimize the tragic fate of

---
(16) Anna Seghers, p. 88.
(17) Anna Seghers, p. 168.

countless persons persecuted for other reasons than socialism.

Although *Das siebte Kreuz* is usually referred to as a KZ novel, the camp itself is never seen in its entirety. The reader sees only the seven crosses on the *Tanzplatz* (so called because the prisoners were forced to do back-breaking exercises there after work), the interrogation room, the torture cells and Commandant Fahrenberg's quarters. The rest of the camp is amorphous and faceless. We learn nothing of the daily life in camp, the struggle to survive in such places. Anna Seghers was mainly interested in showing the compassion and socialist awareness of a large number of inhabitants of her native region. She may have used this part of the country as *pars pro toto* for the German attitude as she believed it to be.

The escape is one of the most unlikely parts of the story, considering the circumstances. We are told of the beatings and torture suffered by Georg Heisler, and we are made to believe that a man, weakened and wounded like Heisler, would be capable of enduring the strain and superhuman effort of such an escape. Even if he were physically able to do this, the author suggests that Heisler immediately after his escape talks and walks with the people of the surrounding country and that they never give a thought to his strange appearance. This happens in spite of the fact that the population is said to have seen prisoners released from the camp and to have been horrified at their cruelly changed appearance.

Due to the above mentioned points of unrealistic treatment *Das siebte Kreuz* is only an exciting escape story with socialist overtones. It stereotypes both the good socialists and the bad Nazis, as the author wishes to see them. The few characters who are given an inner dimension, such as Helwig and the commissioner, are the ones wavering between good and evil. The novel does not come to grips with reality.

Erich Maria Remarque's *Der Funke Leben*,(18) a novel about the political KZ, was published in 1952. Like Seghers, Remarque also spent the years of the NS regime in exile. He too could perceive Germany and specifically the camps only through information gleaned from documentaries, news reports and eyewitness reports. Due to the ten years' difference in publication date from Seghers' book, Remarque had access to post-war documents and reports that considerably facilitated the creation of an authentic setting. There was also for Remarque a sense of *déjà vu* about many aspects of the KZ setting and organization: the enforced proximity under unsanitary conditions, debasement and deprivation of human beings, banding together for mutual support under conditions of stress. Many facets of the KZ life had a strong resemblance to the life in the trenches of the Western front during World War I. Remarque had created a memorial to the men suffering in these trenches in his novel *Im Westen nichts Neues*.(19) Due to his thorough knowledge of the mentality developed under the inhuman conditions of the trenches of World War I, he was able to identify to a large extent with the KZ mentality without personal knowledge of it.

Neither the world of the trenches nor the world of the KZ conformed to the rules of the civilized world and both demanded total realignment of priorities for survival. Remarque's previous experience enabled him to create a convincing account of the camp over and above the facts given in documentaries and reports. Unlike Seghers, Remarque does not portray the world of Germany outside of the camp in great detail. He does not presume to know or

---

(18) Erich Maria Remarque, *Der Funke Leben* (Köln-Berlin: Kiepenheuer & Witsch, 1952).
(19) Erich Maria Remarque, *Im Westen nichts Neues* (first published 1929; rpt. Köln-Berlin: Kiepenheuer & Witsch, 1962).

judge the mentality prevailing in NS Germany, and therefore his outside world is as amorphous and vague as Seghers' KZ world.

The works of Erich Maria Remarque are classified as *Unterhaltungsliteratur*. They therefore never merit more than a passing mention in any literary survey or critique. The well-known essayist and critic Marcel Reich-Ranicki says of him: "Die literarischen Ergebnisse weisen nicht gerade auf einen zwingenden Impuls hin. Und dass weder das Intellektuelle noch das Sprachliche zu den starken Seiten dieses Autors gehören, dass sich hier ... eine beträchtliche handwerkliche Begabung zu Worte gemeldet hatte--konnte schon nach dem Erstlingswerk kaum bezweifelt werden."(20) But in defense of *Unterhaltungsliteratur* it is said by Wolfgang Langenbucher that: "... der Unterhaltungsroman entwickelt sich aus der realen gesellschaftlichen Kommunikation, aus dem aktuell bedingten Gespräch der Menschen untereinander."(21) It would be difficult to think of a German author within the last four decades whose work would come closer to this definition. Remarque's work certainly reflects the "aktuell bedingten" conditions of his time. *Der Funke Leben* does not claim a counterpart in reality as does Bruno Apitz's novel *Nackt unter Wölfen*.(22) Remarque can therefore not be accused of tampering with historical facts to enhance his stories. His "sensationalism" as Reich-Ranicki calls it,(23)

---

(20) Marcel Reich-Ranicki, *Deutsche Literatur in West und Ost; Prosa seit 1945* (München: R. Piper Verlag, 1966), p. 253ff.
(21) Wolfgang Langenbucher, "Unterhaltung als Märchen und als Politik," in *Tendenzen der Deutschen Literatur seit 1945* ed. Thomas Koebner (Stuttgart: Alfred Kröner Verlag, 1971), p. 326.
(22) Bruno Apitz *Nackt unter Wölfen* (Halle a/S: Mitteldeutscher Verlag, 1961).
(23) Marcel Reich-Ranicki, p. 255.

remained purely in the realm of fiction. It served to assure the attention of a wide and varied audience. He entertained his readers, if his novels of the tragic period of the German thirties and forties can be called entertainment. At the same time he created a chronicle in fictionalized form of the many aspects of suffering caused by war and tyranny in 20th century Germany.

As he had portrayed the fate of the German emigrants in *Arc de Triomphe*(24) with compassion and a detailed knowledge of the tragic subject, so he has in this work portrayed some of the most tragic victims of the NS period: the KZ prisoners. Through his aforementioned experience in the trenches of the Western front he was well acquainted with the physical and psychological results of enforced confinement, when men were deprived of the bare necessities and under the constant shadow of death. That knowledge coupled with the information from the available documentaries and reports, such as Wolfgang Langhoff's *Die Moorsoldaten* and Eugen Kogon's *Der SS Staat*(25) appears to have provided the raw material for *Der Funke Leben*.

The setting of Remarque's story is the KZ "Mellern," somewhere in Western Germany. It is a composite of all the real political KZs of the period. The time is the last few days before the liberation of the camp by Allied forces. This period is the same as the one used by Apitz for *Nackt unter Wölfen*. Apitz's account of this period in Buchenwald is highly dramatic in plotline. Remarque dispenses with sensational plot complications. He limits himself to an almost laconic report of the actions and thoughts of the prisoners. The drama is supplied by the

---

(24) Erich Maria Remarque, *Arc de Triomphe* (Zürich, 1946).
(25) Eugen Kogon, *Der SS Staat; das System der deutschen Konzentrationslager* (Frankfurt a/M: Verlag der Frankfurter Hefte, 1946).

background of the approaching Allied forces contrasted by the SS-guards' endeavour to carry on "business as usual." Between these two forces, hope and despair, the prisoners are transported back and forth. They have only one aim: survival; not for revenge, not to be living reminders, but for the mere chance to be free again. The protagonist of the story, 509, phrases it thus: "Man wird vor uns nicht auf die Knie fallen, wenn wir hier herauskommen.... Man wird alles ableugnen und vergessen wollen. Uns auch. Und viele von uns werden es auch vergessen wollen...."(26) Having known life in the trenches, where somewhat similar conditions prevailed, Remarque comprehended better than any other German writer dealing with the subject the basic rule of camp life: social Darwinism in its most elementary form; adapt in order to survive: "Der Kampf um eine Brotkruste war wichtiger geworden als alles andere--und ebenso die Erkenntnis, dass Hass und Erinnerung ein gefährdetes Ich ebenso zerstören können wie Schmerz. 509 hatte gelernt ... sich um nichts mehr zu kümmern als um die nackte Existenz von einer Stunde zur andern."(27) The following lines from *Im Westen nichts Neues,* written more than twenty years earlier show the similarity of the conditions: "Unsere Lage ist zu verzweifelt, um sentimental sein zu können.... Uns bleibt nichts anderes übrig, als sachlich zu sein. So sachlich, dass mir manchmal graut, wenn einen Augenblick ein Gedanke aus der früheren Zeit vor dem Kriege, sich in meinen Kopf verirrt."(28)

The attitude of *Sachlichkeit* extends also to fellow inmates. Lohmann, one of the group of camp veterans in the section reserved for the disabled and dying, offers a gold dental crown to his friends that they may exchange it for

---

(26) Erich Maria Remarque, *Der Funke Leben,* p. 126.
(27) Erich Maria Remarque, p. 15.
(28) Erich Maria Remarque, *Im Westen nichts Neues,* p. 149.

food. The crown has no value to him, he is dying. But for the barely alive friends it might mean one more day's sustenance. The friends accept the gift unhesitatingly and help him break the crown out of his mouth: " ... er war nicht zu retten. Deshalb redeten sie über ihn wie über einen Stein. Die Jahre im Lager hatten sie dazu gebracht, sachlich zu denken."(29) Remarque here has obviously adapted an analogous incident out of his World War I work.(30) The object in question in *Im Westen nichts Neues* is a pair of shoes of a dying comrade. The situation is the same, only the need has taken on a much more cruel intensity in *Der Funke Leben*. The shoes' equivalent becomes a matter of a day's survival for the prisoners. The author has succeeded in portraying the world of the KZ in which all normal rules are suspended and in which the surrealist, nightmarish situations arising daily have to be treated and be dealt with in a factual manner. Here too his previous knowledge aided him in creating an authentic milieu.

One of the valid points emphasized by Remarque is the denial of heroism as a virtue in the KZ. 509, a composite of the intellectual KZ inmates, explains this elementary camp tenet to a younger comrade: " ... und je besser die Männer, umso grösser war oft die Narrheit, wenn sie glaubten, Mut zeigen zu müssen.... Verdammter Lesebuchquatsch ... Bei Widerstand kommt es nur darauf an, was man damit erreicht; nicht wie es aussieht. Sinnloser Mut ist sicherer Selbstmord. Unser bisschen Widerstand ist das einzige, was wir noch haben. Wir müssen es verstecken, damit sie es nicht finden--es nur in äusserster Not gebrauchen...."(31) Remarque's attitude in this matter is reminiscent of Brecht's *Massnahme gegen die Gewalt*

---

(29) Erich Maria Remarque, *Der Funke Leben*, p. 61.
(30) Erich Maria Remarque, *Im Westen nichts Neues*, p. 16.
(31) Erich Maria Remarque, *Der Funke Leben*, p. 124.

in *Geschichten von Herrn Keuner*.(32) Like Herr Egge, 509 submits to the oppressor without a word. His *Nein* to oppressor and oppression has to wait until he has survived the oppressor and oppression. This quasi prescription for survival alone contradicts the judgment of Hansjörg Elster(33) about Remarque. Far from being " ... platte Philosopheme ..." it is a more accurate description of the KZ inmate's mental attitude than the image of the heroic prisoner who unflinchingly faces torture and death.

Like most of his other works, *Der Funke Leben* is another facet of Remarque's lifelong effort to denounce war and political oppression from left or right. His protagonist, 509, is determined to outlive tyranny in its present form and refuses to recognize the need for any other "ism," be it communism or socialism, to replace the evil of fascism. To him they are all the same evil in different disguises. He disagrees with a communist fellow inmate when the latter tries to persuade him that communist rule of post-Nazi Germany would be an improvement. 509's cynical answer to such *Fortschritt* is: "Das ist ein Fortschritt? Wert dafür hier gewesen zu sein...."(34) In spite of being an apolitical pacifist, Remarque had to recognize the documented fact(35) that only the communist ideology was strong enough to serve as a kind of rallying force for any underground action in long established political KZs.

---

(32) Bertolt Brecht, *Prosa II* (Frankfurt a/M: Suhrkamp Verlag, 1965) p. 106.
(33) Hansjörg Elster, "Erich Maria Remarque", in *Handbuch der deutschen Gegenwartsliteratur* ed. Hermann Kunisch (München; Nymphenburger Verlagshandlung, 1965), p. 124.
(34) Remarque, *Der Funke Leben*, p. 309.
(35) Benedikt Kautsky, *Teufel und Verdammte; Erfahrungen und Erkenntnisse aus 7 Jahren in deutschen Konzentrationslagern* (Verlag der Wiener Volksbuchhandlung, 1946), p. 132.

The communist doctrine inspired discipline and cooperation under pressure, but this fact applied only to the communist comrades. Though Remarque recognizes the usefulness of this doctrine in a *Notgemeinschaft* such as the KZ, he foresees that it would result in an enforced *Gemeinschaft*, therefore tyranny, in a free world. This contingency he abhors.

In this as in all his other works dealing with the victims of the NS regime, Remarque does not stress any one religious or political group of victims. They are all suffering individuals, occupied with the fight for survival. They group together in small enclaves for mutual aid and they fight for their small groups against outsiders. One of the veterans from the camp of the dying and disabled says Kaddish for each of the dead from his block: "Es wird ihm nicht schaden ..."(36) and the body will be consecrated by the prayer, regardless of religion. On the other hand the author does not hesitate to confront the reader with a virulent antisemitic tirade from a dying prisoner. Only a few passages serve to point out that the Jewish prisoners in established political KZs, like the fictional camp Mellern, were treated with more intense brutality and more severe deprivations than the other prisoners. This fact is confirmed by Ernst Wiechert's observations on the fate of the Jews in Buchenwald in his book *Der Totenwald* (37). However, Bruno Apitz in *Nackt unter Wölfen,* also set in Buchenwald, omits this fact.

The antagonists, represented by the group of SS-men guarding and administrating the camp, are depicted as one-dimensional stereotypes of evil. They differ only in the individual expressions of their villainy. The gamut runs from the pompous weakling bureaucrat via the vicious sadist to

---

(36) Remarque, *Der Funke Leben,* p. 77.
(37) Ernst Wiechet, *Der Totenwald,* (Zürich: Rascher Verlag, 1946).

the brutal beast, much like Seghers' stereotypes. Remarque, along with other exile writers, may have refrained from giving the antagonists any complex facets so as not to weaken the impact of monolithic evil.

In *Der Funke Leben* Remarque abstains completely from any discussion or judgment of the civilian population of Germany. He singles out the camp, its inmates and its operatives. Thereby he has avoided taking a stand on the German attitude in general during the NS period.

Similar to Seghers' viewpoint, the view of Apitz had also been strongly colored by his adherence to the socialist ideology, when he created his KZ novel *Nackt unter Wölfen*. The material for this novel was based on his eight years as an inmate of KZ Buchenwald. He had been imprisoned there as a leading member of the communist party. Apitz is of proletarian parentage and background and lacks the classical education of the bourgeois.(38) As a dedicated party member since 1927, his artistic abilities are directed towards the glorification of the party. In his novel he has employed them to this end. According to the evaluation in Reich-Ranicki's note on Remarque's work, Apitz's novel should also fall into the category of *Unterhaltungsliteratur*. Metaphorically his language borders on *Kitsch,* and the sensationalism of the plot goes so far as to tamper with historically known facts. However, his work seems to be valued much higher than that in the DDR, since it received the *Nationalpreis* in 1963 and the *Erich Weinert Medaille* in 1966.(39) It must be assumed that these honors were awarded for propaganda value, since neither content nor form approximate the level of Remarque's work.

---

(38) *Lexikon deutschsprachiger Schriftsteller,* ed. Günter Albrecht (Leipzig: Bibliografisches Institut VEB, 1967), p. 40.
(39) Ibid.

Both Bruno Apitz and Ernst Wiechert, another distinguished author of a KZ book, make the distinction between good and bad Germans, much like Anna Seghers. Neither Apitz nor Wiechert condemn all of Germany for its part in the political events. But Apitz's distinction runs along more simplistic lines than Wiechert's. Wiechert, the product of the middle class and a classical education, distinguishes a Germany imbued with the values of a great spiritual and intellectual tradition from the nightmare Germany ruled by madmen claiming to be representatives of their country. Apitz differentiates along party lines: good equals socialist, bad equals Nazi.

The plot of Apitz's novel also deals with the last few days of a KZ before its liberation by the Allied troups. The setting is nonfictional: it is KZ Buchenwald, where death, to use a paradox, had become an accepted way of life. With the approach of the Allied armies, the possibility of life and freedom seems to be within reach. Staying alive has top priority. The battle of wits is joined between the SS and the inmates. The SS is plotting elimination of all incriminating traces and subsequent escape; the inmates are counterplotting to survive until the Allies can liberate them. The points of departure of *Nackt unter Wölfen* and *Der Funke Leben* are identical in time and setting. But here Apitz enhances the already highly dramatic situation with a sensational turn of the plot. The catalyst of this plot is a three-year old child smuggled into Buchenwald in the suitcase of an Auschwitz evacuee in the early spring of 1945. This child of Jewish origin had supposedly been saved from the gas chambers at the age of three months and had been hidden in the barracks of the KZ Auschwitz for nearly three years.

It is true that Jorge Semprun in his autobiographical novel *The Long Voyage*(40) mentions some Jewish children

---

(40) Jorge Semprun, *The Long Voyage* trans. Richard Seaver (New York: Grove Press, 1964) p. 98.

who had arrived at Buchenwald in a transport from a Polish camp and had been gunned down by the SS-guards. But even these children could not have come from Auschwitz. Due to extensive documentation at the time of the publication of Apitz's book it was known that the selections made immediately upon arrival of a transport in Auschwitz eliminated anyone under fourteen and over thirty-five. Leon Poliakov's documentary *Harvest of Hate,* (41) an extensive report on the destruction of European Jews, had been published in 1956. Eugen Kogon's *Der SS Staat* was published in 1946. By 1958 even the reader in the DDR must have known that no three-months old Jewish child could have possibly survived in hiding in Auschwitz for more than a day. By this kind of sensationalism the author weakens his credibility.

Apitz proceeds to make this child the key figure in the struggle between humanity, in the person of the ILK *(Internationales Lagerkommittee),* the communist underground, and inhumanity represented by the SS antagonists. The child serves to add humane aspects to the ILK members who are otherwise only ruled by fierce party loyalty and discipline. One of the child's protectors is an important member of the committee. He is put into solitary confinement for interrogation because of the child and willingly undergoes torture to prevent discovery of the child's hiding place. This child having survived against all odds, becomes a symbol of life and hope, and as such it must be protected at all cost. As a fitting finale, after a pitched battle between the inmates and the SS, the boy is carried off by one of his protectors through the open gates into the rising sun of freedom.

Apitz emphasizes an important facet of his political belief, the intense loyalty inspired by the party in a

---

(41) Leon Poliakov, *Harvest of Hate,* (London: Elek Books Ltd., 1956).

situation of danger. Like Seghers, he too, distorts the truth about the many victims of the regime. There were many non-communist inmates in Buchenwald, as in all the other camps, who managed to survive without being loyal party members. Neither did they: "... sich um persönlicher Vorteile willen als willfährige Subjekte der SS herabwürdigen ..."(42) Three points are heavily underscored in the novel: 1. The importance of the communist party underground organization in the camp; 2. The unmitigated evil of the SS; 3. The all-encompassing humanity of the party members, who manage to combine love for the individual with the interest of the collective.

The first of these points is emphasized repeatedly with such *Kitsch* clichés as: "Ueberall Genossen, die das in Schweigen eingebettete Wissen im Herzen trugen. Die Partei, der sie verbunden, war mit ihnen im Lager, unsichtbar, ungreifbar, allgegenwärtig."(43) Or: "Was an Menschen den Stacheldraht der Konzentrationslager hinter sich lässt, das wird der Vortrupp einer gerechten Welt sein.... Wir sind die Träger der höchsten Pflicht."(44) Apitz was to some extent justified in stressing that the political, mainly communist, structure in the established camps like Buchenwald was of material aid to the inmates who were of similar persuasion. But his ideological bias is obvious.

Secondly, Apitz continues the trend found so frequently carried over from the exile literature during the late forties and early fifties, i.e. the one-dimensional stereotyping of the NS operatives in the camps and everywhere else. For Apitz this method serves to make his heroes look more heroic against the background of the villainous SS. The SS personnel of the novel has only one thought: to escape from the approaching Allies without leaving any

---

(42) Apitz, *Nackt unter Wölfen*, p. 33.
(43) Apitz, p. 42.
(44) Apitz, p. 343.

traces of their regime. Apitz shows the divisive bickering between the stupid faction led by *Kommandant* Schwahl, who opts for evacuation of prisoners, and the vicious faction represented by *Lagerführer* Kluttig, who prefers liquidation of all inmates by force. The ILK furthers this struggle between the factions by playing them out against each other. Thereby they gain time to prepare their uprising. Against the noble humaneness of the ILK members, the stereotyped SS men appear like black painted paper figures.

The third point of emphasis, the humaneness of the communist party members over and above party discipline, is brought out by a sensational *coup de theâtre:* the Jewish child in the suitcase. The is strange that there is no mention made throughout the book of Jewish ILK members. There must have been Jewish communists in Buchenwald. The only mention of Jewish inmates, besides the child, is made in two short sentences about the Jews being chosen as the first group to be evacuated in a last frantic attempt to prevent their liberation by the Allies.(45)

The suspicion arises that the child in question is designated as Jewish so Apitz can show communist compassion for Jews in the person of this child. According to Benedikt Kautsky there was strong anti-Semitism among the non-Jewish prisoners, and the higher camp functionaries were only partly successful in combatting it.(46) This particular plot development seems designed to counterbalance such reports.

It is unfortunate that Apitz could not be content to fashion his novel from verifiable facts. During eight years of imprisonment he must have collected enough material without having to resort to improbable involvements like

---

(45) Apitz, p. 457.
(46) Kautsky, *Teufel und Verdammte*, p. 133.

the Jewish child in the suitcase or the undocumented heroic final battle between SS and the ILK members. Kautsky's work gives details of the liberation of the camp, including the time of day,(47) without once mentioning such a battle. These historic inaccuracies added to the stereotyped good versus evil, personified by party members versus SS, merely contribute to the propaganda value of the work. This is a book peopled by paper cut-outs in black and white.

Like Apitz, Ernst Wiechert wrote his work on the KZ, *Der Totenwald,* from first hand experience. He was one of the few renowned authors who had remained within the borders of the Third Reich. In 1938 he was imprisoned for publicly sympathizing with Pastor Niemöller, a dissenting Protestant clergyman. Due to his prominence and to his influential friends Wiechert was released after one year. He recorded his experience in the form of a third person narration in 1939. For security reasons he kept these writings buried in his garden until the end of the war and published them in 1946.

Der Totenwald was hailed at its publication in Germany and abroad as proof that "Ernst Wiechert is ... ein Bürge von Deutschlands seelischer Gesundheit und politischer Genesung...."(48) F.C. Weiskopf in a book review called it " ... a report from the doorway about events and men seen with the soul - the soul of a sometimes sentimental, warmhearted, highly articulate poet."(49) There was only one dissenting voice among the critics: Max Frisch in an

---
(47) Kautsky, p. 284.
(48) Bayard Quincy Morgan, "Bürge für Deutschland," in *Ernst Wiechert, der Mensch und sein Werk* (München, 1951), p. 234.
(49) F.C. Weiskopf, "Report from the doorway of death," in *Saturday Review of Literature,* XXX, 25 (June 21, 1947), 20.

article in the *Neue Schweizer Rundschau*(50) takes Wiechert to task for "gefährlicher Mangel an Denkkraft, der sich so gerne für Tiefe des Gemüts hält...." He specifically singles out a paragraph in *Der Totenwald* relating to the treatment of the Jews by the NS regime: "Und mochten jene [die Juden] schuldig sein an manchem in der Summe ihres Lebens, mochte das ganze Volk schuldiger sein als andre Völker; hier zerging ihre Schuld in nichts vor der Schuld derjenigen, die sich als das neue Volk priesen. Furchtbarer war niemals gebüsst worden, als jene büssten. Und mehr Schande war niemals auf die Stirne eines Volkes gefallen, als auf jenes, das nun ihre Henker stellte."(51)

Guilty of what? Atone for what? If this were the only expression of sanctimonious prejudice in this book it would be enough to invalidate it as proof of: " ... seelische Gesundheit und politische Genesung ..."(52) of the German artist. But a thorough perusal of the work reveals several passages that sound harshly dissonant with the concept of spiritual health and political recovery.

Arno Schirokauer in his article "Zu Wiecherts Totenwald" unwittingly puts the finger on one of the more jarring discords of this work: " ... die Sprache Wiecherts ... in ihrer blanken Sauberkeit und sicheren Stufung, in hoher Zucht und Weihe der Form macht sie vergessen was an Entsetzlichem sie bezeichnet. Ohne Nachsicht wird Grauenvolles aufgedeckt, aber die Worte, die es enthüllen, legen zugleich die Schleier ihres Adels darüber."(53) It is

---

(50) Max Frisch, "Stimmen eines anderen Deutschland," in *Neue Schweizer Rundschau*, XIII, (1945-46) 537-47.
(51) Wiechert, *Der Totenwald*, p. 99.
(52) Bayard Quincy Morgan, see footnote 48.
(53) Arno Schirokauer, "Zu Wiecherts Totenwald," in *Neue Rundschau*, Jhrg. 1947, 348-52.

precisely the pompous quasi-legendary form of his language coupled with a *Nominalstil* which does not fit the content. Various examples exist in which elevated form is used to satirize base content, for instance in the poetry of Joachim Ringelnatz or Christian Morgenstern. But satire is not Wiechert's intent. His aim is rather to lift this one-time occurrence to the level of universal validity. He therefore envelops the camp's spectres of horror in the richly embroidered gowns of his language. The result is ludicrous instead of tragic or elevated.

Pompous phrases might be overlooked if the work as a whole rang true as the report of a humane writer concerned with crimes against humanity. But the thinly veiled phrases of intolerance and prejudice running through the work give the lie to the repeatedly voiced humane concern. The objectionable passage cited by Frisch would be enough to condemn Wiechert of anti-Semitism disguised in superannuated religious platitudes. These same platitudes are mouthed by Pope Pius XII in Hochhuth's *Der Stellvertreter*.(54) Hochhuth put these words in the mouth of the historical character to point out that character's hypocrisy. Wiechert's lines are spoken by his narrator out of his own conviction. There is also a descriptive passage that is much less veiled: "Auf einer niedergelassenen Pritsche schliefen ... zwei Juden, die leeren Essnäpfe zwischen den Füssen. Sie hoben die unrasierten bösen Gesichter, knurrten eine Frage ... und sanken gleich wieder in einen schnarchenden Schlaf zurück."(55) The spectre of the caricatured Jewish image out of the pages of *Der Stürmer* seems to have been resurrected here.

Anti-Semitism is not the only false note in this work; throughout the pages several anti-Slavic allusions stand

---

(54) Rolf Hochhuth, *Der Stellvertreter* (Reinbek b/ Hamburg: Rowohlt Verlag, 1963).
(55) Wiechert, *Der Totenwald,* p. 62.

out, also tastefully circumscribed, such as " ... die als Geheime Staatspolizei bezeichnet wurden und deren asiatische Methoden mehr Blut und Tränen über das deutsche Volk gebracht haben...."(56) Does Wiechert mean to imply that cruelty and brutality are Asiatic prerogatives? In another passage Wiechert speaks of " ... ein junger Pole, der sein Land verlassen hatte ... und mit der leisen Dumpfheit beschattet, die das Erbteil östlicher Erde ist."(57) This is a circumlocutory way of indicating the inferiority of the Eastern or Slavic nations. Wiechert's intolerance extends even to German inmates of the *Bibelforscher* denomination (Jehova's Witnesses) of whom he says: "Doch lag begreiflicherweise keine beispielgebende Kraft in der Starrheit ihrer Haltung, weil ihre Wurzeln in einen zu dumpfen Boden reichten. Der Märtyrer, der für den Glauben stirbt, dass man nur Gras essen dürfe, begibt sich des Heiligenscheins um seine Stirn."(58) The members of this denomination who remained voluntarily in the camps for the sake of their principles do not deserve such denigration.

Throughout this book the word *dumpf* is found in various places, but always with the same connotation.(59) It invariably implies prejudice against the person or group that it describes.

Unlike Bruno Apitz who only elaborated on certain aspects of the camp as they related to his personages, Wiechert gives a more detailed description of the so-called "everyday life" in Buchenwald and of the almost casual daily tortures and persecutions. He does admit that the experience of his protagonist with the unsubtly symbolic name Johannes (the martyred evangelist) was not as unbearable as

---

(56) Wiechert, p. 12.
(57) Wiechert, p. 65.
(58) Wiechert, p. 129.
(59) Wiechert, ftnt. 57.

that of the average prisoner. For instance: Johannes is ill with a gangrenous arm. He is taken into a separate part of the camp hospital barracks and there he is given extensive treatment, which saves his arm. As he leaves the barracks he observes " ... den sporenbewehrten Arzt bei der Ausübung seines Dienstes. Es war ... verboten, dass sich vor der Revierbarracke mehr als je zehn Kranke ... aufstellten ... so gab es für einen Teil von ihnen keine andere Möglichkeit als sich ... auf die Lauer zu legen und ... herbeizustürzen, wenn eine Gruppe hereingeholt worden war.... Es gab Schwerkranke, die stundenlang dastanden oder kauerten und schliesslich doch umkehren mussten."(60) Johannes ascribes his preferential treatment to the fact that his fellow inmates have recognized in him the well known author who had voluntarily jeopardized his secure position by declaring his allegiance to the dissenting Pastor. He adds, however, that for the same reason he was treated with increased brutality by the SS. This preferential treatment is given to him by the " ... asozialen und verbrecherischen Elementen wie es in den offiziellen Verteidigungen der Lager ... hiess (Der misslungene Hochverrat ist ja immer ein 'Verbrechen', so wie der gelungene eine Ruhmestat ist)."(61) If there remained even a trace of shame in the German people, Wiechert felt it could only be found among these elements, that group of long term political prisoner functionaries mentioned by Kautsky and Amery.(62)

It seems to have taken Ernst Wiechert several years of living under the NS regime to reach the point of feeling the kind of shame expressed by the *asozialen Elemente* in the camp. Even at the beginning of his imprison-

---

(60) Wiechert, p. 122.
(61) Wiechert, p. 144.
(62) See ftnt. 35 and Jean Amery, *Jenseits von Schuld und Sühne* (München: Szczesny Verlag, 1966), p. 17.

ment during the first days of interrogation he still felt sufficiently aloof to believe that " ... des Reiches Schande war nicht seine Schande."(63) Only after being informed by a cellmate about the atrocities committed in the KZs does Johannes, the author's alter ego, acknowledge a sense of shame: " ... Er *wollte* [Wiechert's italics] nicht glauben. Hinter allen Schatten und Flecken im Bilde seines Vaterlandes wollte er immer noch das Ursprungsgesicht sehen, ein einfaches ... gläubiges Gesicht ... Es war ihm als häufe man Schande auf die Namen aller seiner Väter und als bestätige sich hier sein Gefühl aus dunklen Stunden der Vergangenheit, dass er sich nämlich mitunter (sic) seines Vaterlandes schämen müsste."(64) Such admissions of belated shame on the part of this prominent intellectual confirm Ludwig Marcuse's comment on the German intellectuals from 1933 on " ... die unwahrscheinliche Rückgratlosigkeit der talentierten Gelehrten und Künstler, wie sie 1933 zum Vorschein kam und bis heute noch nicht zugegeben wird ."(65)

Wiechert hides his prejudices behind stereotyped religious cliches and pompous *Dichtersprache*. He is openly disdainful of his fellow countrymen who became active Nazis. But the implication, however poetically disguised, remains clear: even the German Nazi is superior to the aliens, meaning Jews and the Slavic people.

For reasons of comparison in viewpoint and manner of treatment of the same events, one of the non-German authors mentioned in the introduction will be discussed in this chapter. The harrowing experiences and the resistance activities leading to imprisonment and torture by the Ger-

---

(63) Wiechert, p. 53.
(64) Wiechert, p. 39.
(65) Ludwig Marcuse, *Mein zwanzigstes Jahrhundert* (Frankfurt a/M: Fischer Bücherei, 1968), p. 149.

mans have been recorded in documentary and fictionalized form by well-known authors of the occupied countries. One of the best foreign language novels to deal with this subject," ... the most complete and original disaster novel ..."(66), is the work of the French writer Jorge Semprun, *The Long Voyage*. Semprun was imprisoned as a resistance fighter while being a member of a French communist underground group. He was deported to Buchenwald in the fall of 1944 where he remained until the liberation of the camp in the spring of 1945. Since the novel deals to a large extent with Buchenwald and the time of action nearly parallels that of Apitz's novel, this work seems well suited to a comparison of the German and the non-German literary interpretation of the KZ.

Semprun uses a complex time scheme to make the long voyage from France to Buchenwald into the central focus of the narration. The central point of *The Long Voyage* is the cattle car. From this point the narration flashes forward and backward in time covering the narrator's whole life until the time of liberation and repatriation. This time scheme has been likened to the time scheme so frequently employed by Marcel Proust.(67) For the purpose of comparison only the parts dealing with the camp itself are of interest. Unlike Wiechert or Apitz, Semprun is neither concerned with atrocities or sensational plot schemes nor with ideologies, political or otherwise. His main concern is the variety of human behavior under inhuman conditions, the utter degradation of some, the dignified acceptance and even moral elevation of others. The book is a first person narrative and the narrator not only recounts the events; it is as if he is trying to explain to himself and anyone who cares to listen the logically inex-

---
(66) A. Alvarez, "The literature of the Holocaust," in *Commentary*, Vol. 37 (Nov. 1964) 65-69.
(67) A. Alvarez, p. 68.

plicable incidents and the reactions of men subjected to them. Small occurrences of the daily camp life described by him give a more authentic picture of the " ... totally unnatural world of the prison of death...."(68) than any details of horror could convey; for instance his description of the new arrivals being shaved in the Sauna (building in which new arrivals were processed):

> At the far end of the room were ten or twelve men in white smocks, with electric clippers.... They were sitting on stools and looked bored to death and shaved us everywhere there was hair.... The shavers worked quickly ... they shaved their men in a trice and it was: All right, next.... Beside me were two little old somewhat misshapen men.... They were watching this circus and their eyes were bulging with disbelief. Their turn came and they began to squeal when the electric clippers went to work on their sensitive parts. They exchanged glances and their expression was no longer of amazement but of holy indignation ... they were grotesque, they were abject....(69)

Semprun immediately grasped the one essential factor of survival: "In order to survive, the organism has to adhere closely to reality and reality was this totally unnatural world of the prison of death."(70) Remarque, though never a KZ inmate, had comprehended the necessity of adaptation to an unnatural world by having survived the unnatural world of the trenches of World War I. Wiechert, though also a soldier in World War I, never recognized the analogous situations of trench war and KZ. His pride in the past greatness of Germany might have prevented him from seeing any aspect which the great past of Germany might have in common with the present dark times. German writers, dealing with the subject (with the exception

---
(68) Semprun, *The Long Voyage,* p. 69.
(69) Semprun, p. 68.

41

of Remarque) have seldom understood or acknowledged that the heroism of the inmates lay in the daily coping with the unrealities of camp life, not in isolated heroics. Semprun phrases it very simply " ... you have to know how to behave and know what the score is. And it's not only a question of dignity, it's also a practical matter. When you know how to act, you have a better chance of holding out (sic)."(71) He goes on to talk about a colonel in the DeGaulle Resistance Movement who was imprisoned with him and who " ... really did not know how to behave. He had stopped washing, he would stoop to anything for a second helping of stinking soup."(72) In such reminiscences Semprun takes the measure of a man much more accurately than through descriptions of ideological loyalties or through words of " ... hohe Zucht und Weihe."(73)

Semprun's language is spare, pared to the absolute basic needs of communication. One feels the reticence of the writer. The more horrifying the situation, the simpler become his words describing it. He talks of a scream heard in the night. Life in the underground, in prison and in camp have taught him to analyze such screams: "The screaming stops short. A nightmare, who knows, they must have shaken the guy. When it's something else, fear, it lasts longer. When it's terror screaming, when it's the idea that you're going to die that's screaming, it lasts longer."(74) When he records the slaughter of some Jewish children brought from evacuated Polish camps in the winter of 1944,(75) his laconic language, almost bare of adjectives, creates an image reminiscent of Picasso's *Guernica*. Insane horror is depicted in absolute basic

---
(70) Semprun, p. 69.
(71) Semprun, p. 137.
(72) Semprun, p. 137.
(73) See ftnt. 53.
(74) Semprun, p. 32.
(75) Semprun, 165ff.

design. Apitz's book-length preoccupation with the fate of one Jewish child appears as maudlin sentimentality by comparison with the three pages in which Semprun condenses the fate of all Jews. Sentences like the following: " ... And the children were running ... and their legs were moving awkwardly slowly and jerkily, as in the old silent film ... and that thing, that pack of dogs and S.S., running behind the Jewish children, soon engulfed the weakest among them, the ones who were only eight years old ... who were knocked down, trampled on, clubbed to the ground ..."(76) stands in stark contrast to Apitz's contrived emotionality, as for instance: "Krämer war zum Kind getreten. Es schaute zu dem grossen ... Mann hinauf mit den samtwarmen Augen eines jungen schönen Tieres, das von den schweigenden Geheimnissen der Jahrtausende mehr weiss als der Mensch."(77)

Where Wiechert and Apitz lift individuals out of the two groups, the inmates and the SS, and make them into stereotypes of the martyr, the stool pigeon, the stupid SS, the vicious SS, etc. Semprun sees these two groups only in terms of "we" and "they." "They" differ decisively from the black cardboard figures of the fifties and early sixties literature in Germany. Semprun is capable of expressing pity for their emotional and spiritual poverty; talking about the execution of a young Russian prisoner before the assembled camp, he says of them: " ... the SS delude themselves into thinking that we are going to experience his death, feel it descend upon us like a threat or warning. But ... we are busy dying this pal's death and by doing so we negate it ... from his death we are deriving meaning and purpose for our lives. A perfectly valid plan for living. But the SS are a sorry lot and never understand such things."(78) He pays repeated homage to the ingenuity of

---

(76) Semprun, 166.
(77) Apitz, p. 57.
(78) Semprun, p. 52.

the human spirit fighting for survival, even with the help of the dead. He describes a macabre ruse of the prisoners to increase their bread rations. They would "... bear the bodies of those inmates who had died in the course of the day out into the square where roll-call was held.... The dead were in the center of the square standing, supported by invisible hands.... With the bread of the dead, the prisoners established a reserve of extra food to help the ill and the infirm.... They helped temporarily at least, to overcome death which constantly stalked the living."(79)

Semprun's novel salutes the heroism of survival and demands a memorial for the ones who did not survive; not a memorial in stone, bronze or words: "These fraternal dead need no explanation. They need a pure fraternal look. What they need quite simply is for us to live, to live as fully as we can."(80) *The Long Voyage* in its laconic language and emotional reticence comes much closer to representing a universal account of man's inhumanity to man than Wiechert's bankrupt classicism or Apitz's sentimental sensationalism.

The foregoing German authors appear to have felt a need for strong stereotyping of the NS operatives. Unlike the younger writers, who were unemcumbered by emotional ties to a great past and flexible enough to be objective, these authors try to rationalize their faith in the continued, uninterrupted decency of their countrymen. Therefore those of their countrymen who had participated actively in the atrocities of the Third Reich had to be represented as types of pure basic evil, without any human facets. Not only could they not belong to the German nation, they could not even belong to the human race.

---
(79) Semprun, p. 209.
(80) Semprun, p. 75.

As the distance between the Holocaust period and the works written about it increases, the German writers of the later decades increase in objectivity to it. They are less and less hampered by pride or nostalgia about the German past. They increasingly deal with people who are good or evil or even both, whether they wear a Nazi uniform or not.

CHAPTER II

THE EXTERMINATION CAMP IN NOVELS AND SHORT STORIES

To define the basic differences between the political KZ and the extermination camp, it is best to defer to the judgment of someone who has experienced both types. Jean Améry,(1) the well-known German philosopher, has had both these experiences. He calls the political KZs the "established camps" where the administration is in the hands of bona fide political prisoners and therefore is structured to benefit, as much as possible, within the limits, the prisoners themselves.

In Auschwitz, the extermination camp, on the other hand, which had been established in 1942 for the main purpose of: " ... bringing about a complete solution of the Jewish question in the German sphere of influence in Europe ..."(2) according to the order given to the then-administrator of the *Protektorat Böhmen und Mähren*, Heydrych, 'day-to-day' improvisation predominated. The inner administration was in the hands of professional criminals and the majority of the inmates were apolitical Jews and Poles interned for sabotage or underground activities. It was probably not incidental, that no politically committed

---

(1) Jean Améry, *Jenseits von Schuld u. Sühne* (München Szczesny Verlag, 1966), p. 17.
(2) Günther Levy, "Pius XII, the Jews and the German Catholic Church," in *The storm over the Deputy,* ed. Eric Bentley, (New York: Grove Press, 1964), p. 202.

prisoners were kept at Auschwitz-Birkenau and thereby a structured administration by the prisoners was prevented. Auschwitz and its annex, Birkenau, the location of the five crematoriums, were not meant for permanent habitations. As opposed to the established camps, which still kept up the myth of "re-education" of political dissenters, Auschwitz and Birkenau were intended to be death factories. The following statistics serve to illustrate the efficiency of this operation:

> It was computed that at Oswiecim [Auschwitz] and the adjacent camp of Brzesinka [Birkenau] alone, more than 1,750,000 Jews from various countries were murdered in the two years ending in April 1944, and at Majdanek nearly 1,500,000.(3)

This does not include the gassing of the Hungarian transports between April 1944 and October 1944, the date of demolition of the gas chambers.

Any *Schutzhäftling,* i.e., anyone imprisoned for the protection and security of the Reich, without a political or criminal record, was automatically destined for the gas chamber. The Germans delivered approximately 10% of each arriving transport into the camp. A small number of these fortunate ones would work in the camp as maintenance workers. The majority went into the free labor pool for the heavy industry conveniently located around Auschwitz and Birkenau. Unsafe working conditions and starvation also delivered these *Schutzhäftlinge* to the gas chambers when they had been drained of their strength.

In such surroundings the unreality and illogic, recognized

---

(3) Cecil Roth, *History of the Jews* (New York: Schokken Books, Inc., 1961), p. 309.

by Remarque(4) and Semprun(5) in the life of the "established" camp, was heightened tenfold. The ability to adapt for survival in it became correspondingly more difficult. Among German fiction writers there seemed to be a marked reluctance to deal with this subject. There were, however, three documentary works which are considered landmarks in Holocaust documentation: Eugen Kogon's *Der SS Staat, Das System der Deutschen Konzentrationslager,* 1946(6), Leon Poliakov's *Harvest of Hate, The Nazi Program for the Destruction of Jews of Europe,* 1956(7) and Hannah Arendt's *Eichmann in Jerusalem, A Report on the "Banality of Evil,"* 1963(8). Arendt's book was influential in pointing the German writers of the sixties into a new direction for the treatment of the topic. A few German dramatists have faced the past in its entirety from that period on. But there is still no major novel dealing with the extermination camp exclusively. Auschwitz or a fictionalized counterpart thereof is used only occasionally in a short story or as a minor part of a whole novel by German fiction writers even after 1963.

One of the first writers to include Auschwitz by name in a fictionalized narrative was Hans Werner Richter in his book *Sie Fielen aus Gottes Hand,*(9) in 1951. The work is a loosely woven narration about the fate of thirteen persons of different nationalities, from the first day of the war, September 1, 1939, until the end in 1945. A camp;:" ... nicht weit von Nürnberg, an der grauen Schot-

---

(4) E.M. Remarque, *Der Funke Leben*.
(5) J. Semprun, *The Long Voyage*.
(6) Frankfurt a/M: Verlag der Frankfurter Hefte, 1946.
(7) London: Elek Books Ltd., 1956.
(8) New York, The Viking Press, Inc., 1963.
(9) Hans Werner Richter, *Sie fielen aus Gottes Hand* (München: Verlag Kurt Desch, 1951).

terstrasse ... "(10) which changes from *Arbeitslager* to KZ to Displaced Persons camp, is the symbolic shadow, that is cast over these lives during the six years of narrated time. This camp becomes the final catchbasin for the thirteen lost souls who dropped out of God's hand. Richter's work is a solemn condemnation of the misuse of power, of brutality, and of war with its dehumanizing consequences. Hans Mayer says of the work:

> ... Richter bemüht sich gleichzeitig um Objektivität und politische Deutung des Geschehenen ... um eine Verbindung des eigentlichen Kriegsgeschehens mit den verursachenden Gesellschaftsfaktoren ... in Deutschland, wie ausserhalb ...(11)

Though Richter belongs to the older generation of writers (he was born in 1908) he did not start his literary activities until after World War II. Unlike his contemporaries Anna Seghers and Ernst Wiechert, he does not separate the NS phenomenon from the continuity of German history. His main concern is with the fate of the individual under the stress of the war events. Herein his point of view is similar to that of Semprun(12) who published his KZ experiences a decade later, and who also stresses the judgment of the individual as his main interest.

In Richter's work the Nazi *per se*, the SS-man, the Gestapo-man, appears for the most part only as a collective that serves as a catalyst for the tragic fate of each of the thirteen individuals. He remains faceless and nameless,

---

(10) H.W. Richter, p. 268.
(11) Hans Mayer, *Zur deutschen Literatur der Zeit; Zusammenhänge, Schriftsteller, Bücher*, (Reinbek bei Hamburg: Rowohlt Verlag, 1967), p. 306.
(12) J. Semprun, *The Long Voyage*.

an impersonal force. Richter, too, did not avoid a slight degree of stereotyping, though the two groups he does type as "good" and "evil" are not the ones the reader would expect to see typed in a German post-World War II novel. Whenever he lifts a German soldier or an SS-man out of the collective, he gives him traits of kindness and moral principles. For instance, the SS-man Willy Gerber, the lover of the Polish partisan fighter Hanja, is executed because he publicly denounces the extermination of Jewish women and children. Slomon, the Jewish cobbler boy, is saved from the burning ghetto when a nameless German soldier advises him to play dead, and then has him taken out of the ghetto under a pile of bodies. At the evacuation from Auschwitz, the men of the *Volkssturm,* guarding the children, Slomon among them, merely chuckle admiringly when the children have the courage to escape from the trucks; they empty their rifles into the air instead of into the escaping children, as they were ordered to do.

At the same time Richter treats the two German nationals belonging to the group of thirteen in his narrative with the least sympathy, and he has very few kind words for individual German civilians within the story. This is a kind of reverse apologism in comparison to other works on this topic coming out of the period; namely, the military and the SS were not all evil but the German civilians were certainly not all innocent. This attitude corresponds to the prevalent mood in Germany before the *Wirtschaftswunder.*(13) Günter Grass in *Die Blechtrommel* has satirized the penitent atmosphere of that period through his protagonist, Oskar Matzerach: "Ich diskutierte mit Katholiken und Protestanten die Kollektivschuld, fühlte mich mit all denen schuldig, die da dachten:

---

(13) Bruno Werner, *Die Galeere* (Frankfurt a/M: G.B. Fischer Verlag, 1958). [-First written 1943-47, Berlin, Strong 'mea culpa' attitude.]

Machen wir es jetzt ab, dann haben wir es hinter uns und brauchen später, wenn es wieder aufwärts geht, kein schlechtes Gewissen mehr haben."(14)

Auschwitz is woven into the narrative of *Sie fielen aus Gottes Hand* through the fate of Slomon, the little Jewish cobbler boy from Warsaw. Slomon is separated from his father at the outbreak of the war. He is taken in by a Polish merchant who passes him off as Catholic and exploits him mercilessly for this favor. When Slomon and his master are caught in an *SS-Aktion,* a roundup of Jews, the merchant denies knowing Slomon and lets him be taken into the ghetto. During the ghetto uprising the underground fighting group he has joined is wiped out. Slomon alone, who is not a *Makkabäer* (a legendary Jewish hero who takes up arms against the oppressor) like the other ghetto fighters is not killed. He survives , thanks to the kindness of the aforementioned soldier. In a phrase strangely reminiscent of Erich Maria Remarque's philosophy in *Der Funke Leben,* (15) Richter expresses through the words of this Jewish child his rejection of heroic values:

> "Hast Du keinen Mut?"
> "Nein," sagte Slomon, "alle die Mut haben, sterben daran."
> "Woher weisst Du das?"
> "Ich habe es gesehen," sagte Slomon.(16)

In spite of the ghetto rescue, Slomon's way leads to Auschwitz, but to an imaginary Auschwitz. Richter has Slomon being interned with hundreds of other children in a children's camp, guarded by *Volkssturm* troops instead of by SS. There was no children's camp at Auschwitz at any time, much less one guarded by kindly

---

(14) Günter Grass, *Die Blechtrommel* (Berlin-Spandau: Hermann Luchterhand Verlag, 1959) p. 540.
(15) E.M. Remarque, *Der Funke Leben,* see ftnt 55, chpt. 1.
(16) H.W. Richter, p. 356.

old men from *the Volkssturm*. It can be surmised that this children's camp served the purpose of the narrative's continuity; it allowed Richter to develop a wistful romance between Slomon and a pathetic little girl named Fanny. The actual facts of Auschwitz, the gaschambers and the crematoriums are only mentioned *en passant*. Since the author at no time hesitates to describe the brutalities of the German army or the German authorities, it must be assumed that he was incapable of visualizing for himself, and thereby for his audience, the absolute depth of brutality as represented by the basic purpose for the existence of Auschwitz.

Slomon, the Jewish cobbler boy, emerges as the *porte-parole* of the author's pleas for peace and compassion among men. But it would seem that Richter is aware of the illusory value of these aspirations. Slomon is the only one of the thirteen main characters who dies a tragic coincidental death after having survived the war. The meek might inherit the heavens, but in our century they do not inherit the earth. It seems an interesting coincidence that Richter's protagonist, the figure of peace and the advocate of life, should be a cobbler just like the protagonist of Nelly Sachs' play *Eli*.(17) Nelly Sachs' play, though written in 1943, was however not published until 1961.

Slomon personifies almost too perfectly all that is humane in Richter's work. In comparison with the other characters he appears one-dimensionally "good." Perhaps Richter was stereotyping the "Jewish victim" consciously, to avoid any reproach of anti-Semitism. The diametrically opposed characterization will be found in the play by Rolf Schnei-

---

(17) Nelly Sachs, "Eli, Ein Mysterienspiel vom Leiden Israel", in Nelly Sachs, *Das Leiden Israel* (Frankfurt a/M: Suhrkamp Verlag, 1965), p. 7-67.

der, *Die Geschichte vom Moischele*. (18) Schneider, to prove his objectivity, gives Moischele every characteristic from heroic to repulsive--with the emphasis on the latter.

The antagonist of Richter's book is actually not a person. Richter uses an interesting device to avoid confrontation with a collective German guilt. The personification of evil is expressed in: " ... jene seltsamen Lager (die) aus dem Boden wuchsen und anfingen sich selbständig zu machen ... Das Lager war ... ein Symbol des dritten Reichs and man hätte es sofort anzünden und vom Erdboden vertilgen müssen bevor es Gelegenheit hatte in eine neue Zeit hineinzuwachsen."(19) The *Lager* is anthropomorphized and looms like "... ein hungriges Tier ..."(20) created for and fed by the victims of power. It will serve any power that feeds it. Richter has, through this manipulation, universalized the culpability of Nazi power hunger to a condemnation of power hunger in any organized society. Even when the *Lager* is used as a shelter for displaced persons after the war, it still retains its ominous aura of evil. It influences its administrators to indulge in dreams of order and regimentation under their control and makes the displaced persons still feel that they are under the shadow of the NS regime that is officially ended.

Though Richter's concept of Auschwitz as a reality is evasive, he has nevertheless managed to condemn the camp, *pars pro toto,* as a menace to individual liberty and the dignity of mankind; as a part of power politics, that must be eliminated before it starts eliminating man. The devices of stereotyping in Richter's work, such as stressing the "good" German in uniform and the "bad" German civilian, are a welcome variation from the previously mentioned clichés, but he creates types

---

(18) Rolf Schneider, *Stücke* (Berlin: Henschelverlag, Kunst und Gesellschaft, 1970), pp. 209-278.
(19) H.W. Richter, p. 467 f.
(20) Richter, p. 470.

nevertheless. In dealing with his country and his compatriots he, too, has not found the kind of objectivity that would let the chips fall where they may.

Heinrich Böll's collection of loosely connected short stories *Wo warst Du Adam* (21) was also published in 1951. Compared with Richter's treatment of the Holocaust particulars, it is still heavily laden with the well-known stereotypes, i.e., when there is a confrontation between Jews and SS it turns into a portrait in stark black and white. Marcel Reich-Ranicki remarks to this tendency: "Sobald Juden als Opfer nationalsozialistischer Verfolgungen erschienen, machte sich sogar bei den vortrefflichen Autoren ein ebenso gutgemeinter wie schliesslich primitiver Philosemitismus bemerkbar. Die in diesen Büchern auftretenden Juden waren - zumindest in vielen Fällen - edel, rührselig und ganz und gar unecht...."(22) There are two consecutive sections in Böll's book that deal with the Jewish persecution. The anti-hero protagonist of the book, a German soldier stationed in Hungary in 1944, meets a Catholic Jewess, Ilona. Their relationship is about to turn into romance. Before a meeting with the soldier that might possibly be the culmination of the affair, Ilona insists on visiting her parents in the German-established ghetto. She is caught in an *Aktion* in the ghetto and is transported to a camp ruled by a commander with the telling name *Filskeit*. This SS-man, Filskeit, loves to select talented singers from the transport for survival, because he fancies himself a connoisseur and gifted conductor of choral music. When Ilona is asked to sing for her life, she intones the Catholic liturgy. This releases a psychotic rage in the SS-man, because he is not only a frustrated musician, he is also filled with terrible love-hate ambiguities toward the Judeo-Christian

---
(21) Heinrich Böll, *Wo warst du Adam?* (Opladen: Verlag Friedrich Middelhauve, 1951).
(22) Marcel Reich-Ranicki, *Deutsche Literatur in West und Ost* (München: Piper Verlag, 1966), p. 222.

love-ethic and toward the feminine sex. The scene ends with the raving mad SS-man commanding the total annihilation of every Jew in the camp.

The Jewess Ilona is beautiful, "edel, rührselig," and totally illogical. Her actions are improbable in view of the high grade of competence and intelligence ascribed to her by the author. In the Hungary of 1944, it is highly unlikely that any Jew who had the protection of a baptismal certificate would venture into the ghetto for a sentimental visit. Böll even has Ilona take her little sister, who is also baptized and therefore safe, with her into the ghetto. Perhaps this plot development served to underline the self-sacrificing devotion of Ilona as the perfection of Judeo-Christian virtues since she was a baptized Jewess. Whatever the case may be, Ilona serves as the perfect foil to heighten the unrelieved depravity of SS-man Filskeit. In the short space assigned to the episode, the many facets of this depravity could only be developed in a very intense one-to-one confrontation with a person who embodied all the aspects that brought out the worst in Filskeit: a beautiful Jewess who sang the liturgy with a superb voice and with the religious fervor of a former nun. The description of the psychotic SS-man losing control in a rage that is mixed with sexual ecstasy is reminiscent of Hollywood's most stereotyped German characterizations during the war movies of the early and middle forties.

As for the description of the camp and its location, it is obvious to a knowledgeable reader that Böll was not too concerned with authenticity in this case. If there were any camps in Hungary itself, they were merely collection points for deportations administered by the Hungarian militia; there was no gassing and no selections undertaken in these camps. In spite of being realistic and detailed with names and places as far as the rest of the hero's odyssey is concerned, Böll was even more vague than

Richter when dealing with the locale of Jewish extermination. He may not have wanted to change the locale of his narrative too drastically for the sake of continuity and therefore he invented the Hungarian extermination camp. The stereotyping in this episode of Böll's *Wo warst Du Adam* is painfully obvious and contrived. No German reader could be remotely expected to identify with a German like Filskeit. This evasion of identification could be suspected as the rationale for the stereotyping of the villains at that period.

In the sixties a new trend and simultaneously a new technique developed in the treatment of this topic. The clearcut division into good and evil was rejected and questions were raised concerning the complicity of all Germans in various degrees. Selectively assembled documents were allowed to speak for themselves. This trend found its strongest exponents in the drama. Where this change of attitude finds expression in fiction, an added innovation can be noted. The omniscient narrator, judge and jury of his characters, has been replaced by several new perspectives: the first person singular narrator; several simultaneous perspectives of the same event; objective narration made up of documentary, scientific observation and fiction. One of the strongest exponents of this technique is Alexander Kluge. He belongs to that generation of writers (born 1932), who were too young during the days of the Third Reich to have to atone for any participation or brainwashing. His style shows objectivity and the detached viewpoint. These writers neither excuse nor accuse, they record. The first attempt at such objectivity can be discerned in Hans Werner Richter's *Sie fielen aus Gottes Hand,* though, as has been noted, the author still employs a traditional narrative form and is prone to stereotypes. These were the techniques common to the older generation.

Alexander Kluge's collection of short stories, *Lebensläufe*,(23) was published in 1962. He introduces the book as follows: "Die Erzählungen dieses Bandes stellen aus sehr verschiedenen Aspekten die Frage nach der Tradition. Es handelt sich um Lebensläufe, teils erfunden, teils nicht erfunden; zusammen ergeben sie eine traurige Geschichte."(24) The saddest of these tales, that "together amount to a sad story," is *Ein Liebesversuch*.(25) The word *Versuch* in this context must be understood as "experiment" rather than as "attempt." The irony of the two contradictory terms "love" and "experiment" seems to set the tenor of this story. Like the other short stories in the volume, *Ein Liebesversuch* is a dry dispassionate record. The story is presented in the form of an interview. The reader has to imagine a newspaperman of the official news agency of the Third Reich (no other newspaperman would be allowed in the vicinity of a KZ) interviewing a fairly garrulous official. The interviewed official, obviously one of the scientists in charge of the experiment, explains his scientific inquiries proudly and verbosely. The "love experiment" had been made, to determine if "unauffällig erzeugte Unfruchtbarkeit ...,"(26) one of the many experimentations conducted in the extermination camps, was effective over a longer period of time. For this purpose two prisoners of the opposite sex, who had been thus sterilized, are kept in close proximity and provided with all available aphrodisiacs, including champagne and soft music. A promise had been given to both the man and the woman that they would not be killed in case of a resulting pregnancy. The scientist makes it clear, however, that such a promise was not intended to be kept. How could science be furthered if the two bodies could not be dissected in case of a pregnancy?

---

(23) Alexander Kluge, *Lebensläufe* (Stuttgart: Henry Goverts Verlag, 1962).
(24) Kluge, *Lebensläufe* Vorwort.
(25) Kluge, p. 133.
(26) Kluge, p. 134.

The scientist had of course chosen his experimental "animals" with care. It had been ascertained that in pre-war life they had been intimate: "Nach den Akten mussten die beiden Versuchspersonen erhebliches erotisches Interesse aneinander empfinden. Insofern unsere Enttäuschung: jetzt durften sie endlich und jetzt wollten sie nicht."(27) The thought that there might be anything resembling conscious resistance or dignity left in these *Versuchspersonen* simply does not enter the scientist's mind. He has taken care of all the physical variables of the experiment and the results should follow accordingly. He is trained to view the *Versuchspersonen* as *Versuchstiere,* not to investigate human reactions, and he obeys orders.

In imitating the official jargon of the Third Reich in this interview, Kluge achieves two things: first he makes the reader aware of the pompous absurdity of the character through evoking derision, thereby eliminating empathy; secondly, with the help of this alienation he lets the reader intellectually absorb the ghoulishness of the situation. By these techniques he effects an unemotional and therefore more severe judgment of a regime producing these absurd murderers than Wiechert with his highflown prose. Even before the appearance of Hanna Arendt's book *Eichmann in Jerusalem*(28) where the phrase "banality of evil" was coined, Kluge recognized that: "Nur die sachliche Konstatierung der Ereignisse konnte ihre sachliche Dimension erfassen. Nur die Berichtform, die Tatsachen nicht in einer ideellen Dimension neutralisierte, gab Argumente in die Hand, ihren 'realen' d.h. gesellschaftlichen Bezug zur Gegenwart herzustellen."(29)

---

(27) Kluge, p. 134.
(28) Hannah Arendt, *Eichmann in Jerusalem, A Report on the Banality of Evil* (New York: Viking Press, 1963).
(29) Frank Trommler, "Der zögernde Nachwuchs," in *Tendenzen der deutschen Literatur seit 1945,* ed.

Like most of the stories in *Lebensläufe, Ein Liebesversuch* is also openended. It ends with a question:

> Was geschah mit den Versuchspersonen?
> Die widerspenstigen Versuchspersonen wurden erschossen.
> Soll das besagen, dass an einem bestimmten Punkt des Unglücks Liebe nicht mehr zu bewerkstelligen ist? (30)

Kluge skillfully demonstrates his point about the *Doppelleben* of many NS Germans. He lets the interviewed scientist use a typically officialese jargon to achieve this effect. Hans Mayer sees this point as the dominant tragedy of the Germans: " ... Aufteilung des Deutschen in den Familienvater und den Beamten ... Musikfreund und Befehlsempfänger. Fülle der Selbstentfremdungen, die niemals zulassen, dass ein 'ganzer Mensch' in Erscheinung tritt und tätig wird."(31) Mayer's interpretation has answered or at least thrown some light on Kluge's "... Frage nach der Tradition ..."(32) This form of habitual self-alienation allowed the Germans to function as they did in positions such as the scientist in question.

Kluge has taken a large step forward in the process begun by Günter Grass in *Die Blechtrommel(33)*: the satiric debunking of the daemonic Nazis in favor of revealing the *Spiessbürger* in uniform. Kluge's satire lies not in his own observation but in letting the material used speak for itself. Form and content of the interviewed scientist's language create a larger-than-life caricature of a still existing type. The reader cannot help but recognize in

---
(30) Kluge, p. 136.
(31) Hans Mayer, p. 342.
(32) Kluge, see ftnt. # 22.
(33) Günter Grass, see ftnt. # 14.

this perpetrator of inhumanities a man who might live next door to him anywhere in Germany.

The same literary device used immediately after the war by German writers to avoid identification with the causes and the perpetrators of the Holocaust, namely creating evil cardboard stereotypes, was also used by some foreign post-war writers when dealing with the same topic. Their stereotyping, however, went one step further. They stereotyped the whole nation to set them apart from the society of men. The books written after the war by non-Germans are mostly fictionalized accounts of personal experiences. During the first decade after the war, this attitude was not only understandable, but unavoidable. Semprun had noted in his work about the KZ Buchenwald that memories of such horrors have first to be buried "in willful oblivion"(34) and then brought back again after many years, so that the writer can achieve objectivity towards them. This he did. But not every writer could, or even wanted to attain such a degree of objectivity. There were those who were only too glad to exploit the wave of shock that had overwhelmed the world after the first full disclosure of Nazi horrors. The worst example of this kind of stereotyped fiction is to be found in a book called *House of Dolls*.(35) It was written by a former Jewish inmate of Auschwitz, Karol Cetynski, who used a pseudonym that guaranteed authenticity, Ka-Tzentnick 135 633. In this type of writing, patently directed towards a sensation hungry public, every male German is a sadistic brute and every female German a depraved pervert. Even the German prisoners are depicted as depraved as their masters, only with less power. The book deals with the supposedly factual military brothel in Auschwitz, staffed

---

(34) J. Semprun, *The Long Journey*, p. 126.
(35) Ka-Tzetnick 135 633 (pseudonym for Karol Cetynski) *House of Dolls* (London: Federick Muller Ltd., 1957).

by Jewish *Feldhuren*. There was such an institution in the Auschwitz compound, but certainly not for the use of military personnel, since the Nürnberg racial laws strictly interdicted such practice. The brothel was for the convenience and as a reward for so-called privileged prisoners, for the elite of the Auschwitz hierarchy. In Eugen Kogon's documentary *Der SS-Staat,* under *Bordelle im KL,*(36) information is cited concerning the establishment of brothels in Buchenwald, Sachsenhausen, Dachau and Mauthausen in 1943. According to Kogon these institutions were staffed with professional prostitutes from the women's camp Ravensbrück. These women volunteered for the jobs after having been promised release from the camp after six months tours of duty. No Jewish women were among the brothel personnel. Besides having falsified the basis for the story, the whole book abounds in falsifications that gratify the prurient taste for sadism and sexual perversions. At the same time the reader is given a chance to feel virtuously compassionate while reading of the suffering of every Jewish woman at the hands of the Nazi brutes and the persecution of every emaciated, handsome Jewish male by sex-starved blondes. These distasteful distortions were briefly successful in the immediate post-war era *House of Dolls* with its pornographic exploitation of the Holocaust had twelve editions within two years.

Fortunately, such commercial exploitation of the Holocaust was short-lived. By 1960 two works had appeared which will take their place in literature as classic works about the extermination camps: Elie Wiesel's *Night* (37) in French and Tadeusz Borowski's *This Way for the*

---

(36) Eugen Kogon (München: Karl Alben Verlag, 1946), p. 148-150.
(37) Elie Wiesel *Night* (New York: Hill & Wang, 1960), translated from the French by Stella Ridway.

Gas, Ladies and Gentlemen.(38) Eli Wiesel was thirteen years old when he came to Auschwitz in 1944 in a Hungarian transport at the height of the Hungarian mass deportations. Borowski, a Polish university student, was sent to Auschwitz as a political prisoner sometime after the German occupation of Poland. The difference in the viewpoints of the two narratives is based on the respective prisoner status of the authors. Wiesel, a child, was a *Schutzhäftling,* which meant in Auschwitz parlance a prisoner without a previous political or criminal record, merely deported for extermination. Only through accident of selection did he come into the camp and was subject to gassing at the whim of the administration. Borowski was a young adult at the time of his incarceration. He had been in the Polish resistance and was well versed in the art of survival under stress. He was a political prisoner, meaning he had a record, and a sentence had been pronounced on him by a court. He therefore could not be exterminated arbitrarily. Also the political prisoners had the privilege of receiving food packages from home, if they still had a home, and therefore of course had the advantage of physical strength. Borowski was never caught in the terrifying struggle against starvation and disease that preoccupied the *Schutzhäftlinge* to the exclusion of everything else. In the years he spent in Auschwitz, he was for these reasons able to observe not only himself, but the camp as a whole, in its social structure.

Wiesel, like Semprun, let a long time elapse before committing his experiences to paper. This allowed for the maturing of his artistic ability and let him achieve the necessary distance from the painful memories so he could offer them to a reading public. Of his camp experiences

---
(38) Tadeusz Borowski, *This Way for the Gas, Ladies and Gentlemen* (New York: Viking Press, 1967), translated from Polish by Barbara Vedder. [First published in 1959 in Wybor Opowiadan, Panstwowy Instytut Wydoniczy.]

between Fall 1944 and April 1945, the end of the war, he has only recorded memories concerning himself and those nearest to him: his father, a few fellow-deportees from his home town, and two male friends in the camp. Throughout the book, Wiesel, the narrator, castigates himself for having felt immense relief, nothing else, at the death of his father. This feeling, combined with the loss of faith in a God who permits such things to happen, is an unbearable burden of guilt on this child reared in a pious Jewish tradition. The author verbalizes the resentment of the child against his elders who precipitated death and suffering for themselves and for him by their refusal to heed the warnings given them of the *Endlösung* in action. Neither a fellow townsman who had miraculously escaped from a *Sonderaktion,* nor a faithful Christian servant who offered a safe hiding place, could deter Wiesel's father, one of the most influential Jewish men in the little town of Sziget, from trusting the "civilized" Germans more than the warnings by interior Jews or by Hungarians. Remarks like: "The ghetto was not guarded. Everyone could come and go as they pleased. Our old servant Martha came to see us ... she begged us to come to her village where she could give us safe refuge. My father did not want to hear of it,"(39) are indicative of Wiesel's resentment and subsequent guilt feelings. In camp this resentment grows with increased deprivation. He finds two young friends with whom he feels a common bond in the fact that " ... their parents, like mine, had lacked the courage to wind up their affairs and emigrate while there was still time."(40)

The memory of the child Elie can only recollect guns, boots, uniforms, and sticks as representing the oppressor. He has no face for him, he is only the featureless cause of his fate. The adult writer Wiesel does not bother to

---

(39) Wiesel, p. 3.
(40) Wiesel, p. 58.

search for individual human faces among this cause. He is only concerned with the effect of this cause on him, and the sins it forced him to commit against God and against his father. He gives all Germans the undifferentiated mask of evil that is found in the immediate post-war works of non-German authors when they discuss the Holocaust period.

In *This Way for the Gas, Ladies and Gentlemen* Tadeusz Borowski writes about the daily life in Auschwitz. He writes as calmly about the horrors as about the few funny moments that occurred in the "asshole of the world."(41) The world of the extermination camp was as structured and as complex as the world of the living, only every aspect of this life was distorted by the threat of death. The complexity of this life was increased by the fact that in Auschwitz men's camps and women's camps existed side by side and a certain amount of furtive contact between the sexes occurred. This fact differentiated Auschwitz' structure from the structuring of the political KZ whose inmates were of one sex only. Like Semprun, Borowski also stresses that the ability to accept these conditions and to concentrate all faculties on functioning in this world spelled the difference between life and death.

Climbing the ladder of success through connections was as much a fact of life in Auschwitz as in the outside world. Only in the camp world, lack of success meant not lack of esteem, but starvation and death. In the outside world everything was available to the rich and the influential; the same held true for the camp's society. But wealth had a different meaning. For the political or administratively employed prisoner it meant one of two things: either he received food from home, with which to barter for

---

(41) Peter Weiss, "Die Ermittlung," in Peter Weiss *Dramen 2* (Frankfurt a/M: Suhrkamp Verlag, 1968), p. 156.

luxuries like cigarettes, clothes or liquor, or it meant the rations he withheld from the less fortunate prisoners in his control, for the purpose of such barter. As the rich man is able to cluck sympathetically about those less fortunate than he, so the well-established prisoner could be occupied with a Sunday soccer game and notice that outside of the fence, where the transports were arriving "... between the throw-ins in a soccer game, right behind my back, three thousand people had been put to death."(42) For these prisoners the daily life passed with pedestrian regularity inside the camp. The narrator talks about reading a book by Pierre Loti "while the procession continued on and on along both roads,"(43) the road to the crematorium and the road to the camps.

The surreptitious kindness of one SS-guard is noted as calmly as the gratuitous beating given gy another guard for no reason at all. The reader learns of the many subterfuges used by the men who work on the roads and in the fields for conserving their small reserves of energy: "The men do not work with their hands but with their

---

Original quotation in a diary kept by Dr. Hans Kremer, professor of Münster University and Hauptsturmführer of the SS ....

September 5th Present this afternoon at a special action from the women's camp (Mussulmen), the worst I have ever seen. Thilo, the medical officer for the troops was right when he told me this morning we are at *anus mundi* ....

as cited in Gerald Reitlinger, *The Final Solution, The Attempt to Exterminate the Jews of Europe, 1939-1945,* Second Revised and Augmented Edition (South Brunswick, N.Y.: Thomas Yoseloff, 1961), p. 124.

(42) Borowski, p. 64.
(43) Borowski, p. 64.

eyes. As soon as an SS-man or the Kapo appears ... the clatter of the spades grows a bit more lively. But whenever possible the spades swing up and down empty.(44) The narrator, a political prisoner, notes with satisfaction that he, like most political non-Jewish prisoners, is better dressed than the SS-guards in their army issue uniforms. Like most influential established prisoners, he has his prison uniforms tailored for a price at the camp tailorshop *(Nähstube)*. All those who were inside the camps appreciated the one relative advantage they had: they were in "a concentration camp--but alive."(45) Staying alive was the main occupation. But having achieved the relative security of an in-camp job and connections, these fortunate prisoners used position and connection to indulge in any available luxury. It was a *carpe diem* attitude. There was no security, one grabbed daily what one could. A whim of the authority could end not only privileges, but life, tomorrow.

Borowski shows the reader all phases of the camp, including the most infernal part of it: the arrival and selections of transports at the railroad ramp where the able-bodied were sent down one road, to the camp, and those under fourteen and over thirty-five down the other road, to the gas. The title story of the book describes a working day at the ramp. This description contradicts Wiesel's description of the cruelty displayed by the prisoner workers at the ramp who had cursed Wiesel's group and told them what was waiting for them.(46) Here is Borowski's description of such a scene:

> They jump from the train ... anxious ...
> "What's going to happen to us?"
> They repeat the question stubbornly gazing into our tired eyes.

---
(44) Borowski, p. 43.
(45) Borowski, p. 64.
(46) Wiesel, p. 40.

> "I don't know."
> It is the camp law: people going to their death must be deceived to the very end. This is the only permissible form of charity.(47)

The inferno at the ramp is described in dry, almost disconnected sentences. The words create an impression more tangible in sight, sound and smell than Hochhuth's elaborate *mis-en-scene* with Schillerian dialogue: " ... freight cars roll in, the heaps of clothing, suitcases and bundles grow, people climb out, look at the sun, take a few breaths, beg for water, get into the truck, drive away. And again freight cars roll in, again people.... I go back inside the train; I carry out dead infants; I unload luggage; I touch corpses...."(48) Borowski does not hesitate to write about the fact that people got used to the camp. The worst horrors occurred at the arrival. If one survived the first few months, one became inured: "The camp inmates had problems of their own: they waited for packages and letters from home, they 'organized' for their friends and mistresses, they speculated, they schemed. Nights followed days, rains came after the dry spell."(49) To the ones who had managed to stay alive and make connections, this nightmare had become the world they lived in. To them the outsiders, the newcomers, were the abnormal ones, they who:

> ... look upon it as something inexplicable ... abnormal something beyond human endurance.
> Today, having become totally familiar with the inexplicable, the abnormal, having learned to live on intimate terms with the crematorium, the itch and tuberculosis ... having

---

(47) Borowski, p. 17.
(48) Borowski, p. 25.
(49) Borowski, p. 77.

> understood the true meaning ... of slavery and power; having so to say broken daily bread with the beast--I look at civilians with a certain indulgence, the way a scientist regards a layman ....(50)

On of the short stories contains references to the much sensationalized brothel from the book of Ka-Tzetnik, *House of Dolls*. But it is here given the correct designation: the *Puff* for the Camp Elders, the Camp Kapos, the prisoner doctors and the Kapos from the Kommandos, as reward for good conduct and diligent work. Far from being forced into the *Puff*, many women vied for the job, as it provided steady admirers and many luxuries. In regard to this pragmatic attitude to survival Borowski also counters in brief the smug reproaches frequently voiced in the post-war era, about the lack of resistance and the "self-abasement of the persecuted, the inclination to conform and even to cooperate with brute force ... wishing to survive, even at the price of self-degradation."(51) "Despite the madness of war we lived for a world that would be different. And perhaps our being here is a step toward that world.... It is that very hope that makes people go without a murmur to the gaschambers, keeps them from risking a revolt.... It is that hope that compels a man to hold on to one more day of life because that day may be the day of liberation...."(52) Just as Borowski sees no need to stereotype the prisoners as totally virtuous so he does not need to stereotype the SS by any specific description. The situations he describes dealing with the SS speak for themselves:

---

(50) Borowski, p. 91.
(51) W.R.S. "Reading Suggestions," in *New Polish Publications,* 5, May 1971, 3.
(52) Borowski, p. 102.

> ... they are dragging an old man wearing tails and a band around his arm ... he moans and wails in an uninterrupted monotone. 'Ich will mit dem Herrn Kommandanten sprechen'
> ... thrown on the truck, trampled by others, choking, he still wails: 'Ich will mit dem ...'
> 'Look here old man,' a young SS man calls, laughing jovially, 'in half an hour you'll be talking with the top commandant. Only don't forget to greet him with 'Heil Hitler.'(53)

In a philosophical excursus he sees the events in the Third Reich camps in the historical context of the eternal price paid by slaves for the building of civilizations:

> Antiquity - the tremendous concentration camp, where the slave was branded on the forehead.... It is we who built the pyramids ... while they rationalized their intrigue by appeals in the name of the Fatherland .... If the Germans win the war, what will the world know about us? ... We shall be forgotten, drowned out by the voices of the poets, the philosophers.... They will produce their own ... virtue and truth.(54)

Borowski does not, as Milton Halprin accuses him, "indict the victims."(55) He indicts the nation that allowed a system under which human beings were forced to adopt the "concentration camp mentality"(56) for survival.

---

(53) Borowski, p. 26.
(54) Borowski, p. 111.
(55) Milton Halprin, *Messengers from the Dead, Literature of the Holocaust* (Philadelphia: The Westminster Press, 1970), p. 111.
(56) Borowski, p. 102.

Reviewing the book at the time of its English publication in 1967, Simon Gray called it "an oblique commentary on the negotiations we conduct daily in our civilized ways."(57)

That a record of the daily life in the "asshole of the world" of the Third Reich is seen as a commentary on everyday life should be noted by German writers. In their effort to oversimplify and to dissociate themselves and their readers from this particular phase of the German past, they overlooked a highly multifaceted source of material. The book about the people who "lived" in Auschwitz could still be written by a German writer.

Another aspect of the Holocaust that has never been touched on by German literary circles is the unique institution *Theresienstadt*. This little 18th Century walled town, close to the German-Czech border, was used by the Nazis as a Potemkin village. Neither all ghetto nor all KZ, it was a carefully arranged stage set of a "protected" Jewish town. This set could be unveiled, whenever the pressures from humanitarian international organizations became too strong and inspection demands could not be avoided. It had all the appearances of a central European small town: the obligatory coffeehouse, concerts, theater, park, etc., down to stores and a bank. The stores and the bank were dummy fronts and the coffeehouse was peopled at certain hours of the day by command. For the cursory inspection, however, it presented all the aspects of a carefree little town, not even remotely resembling the images of the horror-propaganda spread among the Allies about the camps. The reverse of the coin was disease, starvation and hard labor, only somewhat mitigated by the efforts of the *Judenrat* to maintain at least the spiritual welfare of the inhabitants.

---

(57) Simon Gray, "A Man of Style," in *The New Statesman*, 622, May 5, 1967.

There were no gas chambers, but that did not mean that all Jews deported to Theresienstadt escaped them. The town was used as a transit camp to Auschwitz for thousands of German, Czechoslovakian and Austrian Jews. For the few hundred privileged Jews who were selected to remain in Theresienstadt, it meant a much better chance of survival. These privileged few were allowed to stay together with their families at least during the day. The young people therefore had a chance to help their parents and the parents could protect their children to some extent. A very minimal percentage of Jews were thus spared the brutal *Endlösung,* or at least were allowed to die a natural death.

There are three sensitive and knowledgeable works of fiction about Theresienstadt written in Czech. Two of them, *Night and Hope(58)* and *Diamonds in the Night(59)* are by Arnost Lustig; *Theresienstädter Requiem(60)* is by Josef Bor. Both of Lustig's works are collections of short stories about life in Theresienstadt. *Night and Hope* deals with the lives of a group of boys in a so-called *Kinderheim*. *Diamonds in the Night* touches all aspects of Theresienstadt, the young, the old, the German administration of SS-man, the Judenrat and more. Bor's work is a narrative about the rehearsal and final performance of Verdi's *Requiem* in Theresienstadt with the help of the finest Jewish artists in Czechoslovakia and Austria, all inhabitants of Theresienstadt. The single-minded devotion of the conductor and the performers in rehearsing the *Requiem* and bringing it to

---

(58) Arnost Lustig, *Night and Hope* (London: Hutchinson of London, 1962), translated by George Theiner.
(59) A. Lustig, *Diamonds in the Night* (Prague: Artia 1962), translated by Iris Urwin.
(60) Josef Bor, *Theresienstädter Requiem* (Leitersloh: Siegbert Mohn Verlag, 1966), translated by Elizabeth Borchardt.

performance against all harassment and difficulties is a tribute to the strength of the Jewish spiritual and intellectual values, which affirm life and beauty in the face of death.

There is as much documentary material and information about Theresienstadt as there is about Auschwitz, but again no German writer has ever investigated this paradoxical milieu for literary exploitation.

The literary treatment of the Holocaust period by foreign established writers like Semprun, Wiesel and Borowski is proof that fiction can be created about the concentration and extermination camps without stereotyping persons or places.

CHAPTER III

THE EXTERMINATION CAMP IN THE DRAMA

Postwar novelists have treated the political KZ and the extermination camp within their works about the Third Reich period, but no major German novel is devoted exclusively to the topic. However in the early sixties the *Endlösung* with all of its ramifications became the main theme for several young German dramatists. The Eichmann trial in 1960-61 and the subsequent Frankfurt trials seem to have been eye-openers for many young Germans. A letter addressed to the President of the *Deutscher Bundestag* expresses this emotional revelation as follows: "Der Fall Eichmann hat uns die Schuld nun doch vorstellbar gemacht, die in unserem Namen begangen worden ist, vorstellbar in ihrem 'unvorstellbaren' Ausmass, in ihrer Ursache, ihren Mitteln, ihrem Vollzug."[1] What Kogon had documented in *Der SS Staat* in 1946 was turning from dry statistics into reality.

The publication of the trial record, combined with the malaise felt by young writers at the complacent basking of the German nation in the glow of the *Wirtschaftswunder* might have been the impetus for the documentary plays, designed to shake this complacency. An American critic analyzes this period as follows: "The Germans would love to get back to 'normal' life and to be unequivocally trusted by their allies in NATO, but all sorts of young Germans themselves, like Rolf Hochhuth (born 1931), are outraged by the claim to bourgeois respectability on the part of so many people, who twenty

---

[1] Frank Trommler, "Der zögernde Nachwuchs," in *Tendenzen der deutschen Literatur seit 1945*, ed. Thomas Koebner (Stuttgart: Alfred Kröner Verlag, 1971), p. 77.

years ago were robbing, torturing and killing all over Europe."(2) The documentary drama in Germany is not only an outgrowth of epic drama, which originated in Germany in the twenties, as is asserted by Jack D. Zipes,(3) but it can be traced much farther back in German literature. One could actually term Schiller's description of the deportation of the indentured peasants to America in Act II, scene 2 of *Kabbale und Liebe* (1784) as partly documentary drama. Büchner's *Danton's Tod* (1826) contained whole speeches from the records of the French National Convention as recorded by Michelet and Thiers; Gerhardt Hauptmann's *Die Weber* is equally part of the ancestry of documentary drama in Germany. Through the years German dramatists had frequently felt compelled to provoke a complacent audience into facing social or political issues. The period of the Nazi Regime, 1933-45, forced a hiatus in this trend. But in the sixties the young German dramatists felt again the need for the provocation of their complacent countrymen.

The first author to attract worldwide attention, flattering as well as unflattering, was Rolf Hochhuth. His documentary play *Der Stellvertreter,(4)* based on several years of careful research into the records of the Vatican State as well as in German Foreign Office records, dating back to the last years of the NS Regime, deals with the *Endlösung* in connection with the Italian Jews and the then reigning Pope, Pius XII. This author did something that was unheard of until that time: he not only accused the Third Reich for its extermination

---

(2) Alfred Kazin, "The Vicar of Christ," in *The storm over The deputy,* ed. E. Bentley (New York: Grove Press, 1965), p. 104.
(3) Jack Zipes, "Documentary Drama in Germany, Mending the Circuit," *Germanic Review,* XLII, 1967, 49-62.
(4) Rolf Hochhuth, *Der Stellvertreter* (Reinbek bei Hamburg: Rowohlt Verlag, 1963).

policies, but Catholic Christianity in the figure of Pius XII, for complicity. Passive complicity of the free world had been tacitly ignored until then. Only in highly secret documents had there ever been any acknowledgement of this fact. According to Leon Poliakov: " ... the International Red Cross refrained from denouncing massacres in the death camps, for fear that to do so would deny it access to civil internment and prisoner-of-war camps and justified its silence on the ground that it had no legal or traditional basis, no international convention, permitting it to intervene. *(Rapport du Comité International de la Croix Rouge pendant la seconde guerre mondiale,* Geneva 1947, vol III, p. 559). Thus official consciences salved their silence."(5)

Though Hochhuth's play had its first performance in the beginning of the sixties, it does not yet contain the detached objectivity that was to be the hallmark of the sixties in drama and fiction, especially as it concerned the Holocaust topic. Hochhuth has written a classic drama in the Schillerian manner; his characters are types, not individuals. Ricardo Fontana, the protagonist, and the Doctor, the antagonist, are stereotypes that belong to the Schillerian dramatic tradition. Ricardo is the hero who, though conquered by fate, deprives evil of its final victory through his death. The doctor is a composite of E.T.A. Hoffmann's daemonic villainy and Goethe's Mephistophelian wit, brilliance and amorality. The Jews depicted in the play, especially in the fifth act, are stereotyped as faceless victims without individuality or personal complexity. The fifth act brings the protagonists and the antagonists into a climactic confrontation in Auschwitz before a background of groveling, whining Jewish victims. On the protagonists' side one finds not only Ricardo Fontana, who has voluntarily accompanied a

---

(5) Leon Poliakov, "Pope Pius XII and the Nazis," in *The storm over The deputy,* ed. E. Bentley (New York: Grove Press, 1965), p. 230.

transport of Italian Jews to Auschwitz, but also the SS-man Kurt Gerstein, a man who claimed to have joined the SS as a "spy for God" so he could reveal the horrors of the *Endlösung* to the world. Gerstein, as a chemist, was forced to perfect Cyclone B gas for the exterminations; the fifth act finds him too in Auschwitz on official business and he attempts to free Fontana through a ruse. The Doctor and the representatives of German industry, the former working as a camp doctor in Auschwitz, the latter having come to inspect their slave labor industries, are the antagonists. The drama is played out in philosophical dialogues between the Doctor and Fontana. In an obvious analogy to Lucifer, the fallen angel, the Doctor feels compelled to disprove the existence of God by challenging Him through ever increasing evil to a demonstration of His existence. Fontana, by his gesture of solidarity with the victims, has publicly disclaimed the Pope, his superior, as a mundane political facsimile of Christ's true deputy. He now attempts to reassert his faith in the basic Christian fundamentals of love and compassion against the sophisticated taunts of the Doctor.

The verbosity of this act is its greatest weakness. The reader and the audience are expected to believe that the forecourts of the gas chambers in Auschwitz could be the location of an intellectual debate in which Valéry and Stendhal are quoted casually, and Nietzschean philosophy could be discussed as to its applicability to the situation. The figure of the Doctor is authentic: the physical description used by Hochhuth corresponds exactly to that of Dr. Mengele, one of the camp doctors. But giving him the aforementioned daemonic characteristics has made Hochhuth's Doctor an incongruous and unbelievable figure in the cast of the extermination camp officials. Throughout the play Hochhuth gives lengthy stage directions and character descriptions in the manner of George Bernard Shaw. In Act V he gives an accurate description of the kind of *"kleiner Beamter"* that was typical for the officialdom of the extermination camps: " ... säuerlich

charaktervolle Bürger, gemäss der unbestreitbaren Feststellung des Fürsten Talleyrand, dass ein verheirateter Mann, der Familie hat, stets bereit sei, für Geld alles zu tun - 'wem Gott ein Amt schenkt, schenkt er auch Kollegen ....' Die Herren sind uns ... obwohl 'erfunden' ... bekannt ... bekannt sind sie uns längst, ob wir sie täglich auf der Rutschbahn ins deutsche Wirtschaftswunder erblikken, oder im Spiegel des eigenen Badezimmers."(6) In most books touching on the Holocaust past, such as Martin Walser's *Halbzeit(7)*, Paul Schallück's *Engelbert Reinecke(8)* or Johanna Moosdorf's *Nebenan(9)*, the criminal past of the solid *Wirtschaftswunder* citizen is seen only in flashbacks. Hochhuth reverses the process: he shows the audience these "average" citizens in the midst of their crimes and flashes forward to their present day respectability. Unfortunately the *"säuerlich charaktervolle Bürger"* never steps on the stage in a major role. By accentuating the daemonically intellectual Doctor, Hochhuth achieves the traditionally correct figure of the dramatic antagonist. At the same time, however, he destroys the true view of Auschwitz as a 24-hour death factory, peopled by little officials, which he so aptly described in his stage directions. In the same act Hochhuth depicts the Jews in oversimplified fashion as the "victims." For example, Carlotta, the Italian Jewess, had been converted and was engaged to an Italian Catholic; she expected therefore to be exempt from deportation. She is nevertheless deported in the same transport with Father Ricardo from Italy to Auschwitz. After one week in Auschwitz, she is portrayed as having forgotten her past with its conflicting emotions of loyalty between her family and her fiancé. Neither does she give

---

(6) R. Hochhuth, p. 184.
(7) Martin Walser, *Halbzeit* (Frankfurt a/M: Suhrkamp Verlag, 1960).
(8) Paul Schallück, *Engelbert Reinecke* (Frankfurt a/M: Fischer Verlag, 1961).
(9) Johanna Moosdorf, *Nebenan* (Frankfurt a/M: Suhrkamp Verlag, 1961).

any thought to having betrayed her Jewish faith and heritage in vain. She is given, instead, all the attributes of a born *Untermensch* without dignity or even the basic instincts of moral preservation. After this short period in camp she is depicted as already sliding on her knees and whining at the injustice of her fate. Even in Auschwitz it took several months for the weakest prisoner to be reduced to whining. Semprun phrased the necessity of preserving a last shred of dignity in precise words: "... you have to know how to behave.... When you know how to act, you have a better chance of survival." (10) Hochhuth had obviously researched most of his information correctly, except that concerning actual conditions and prisoner mentality in Auschwitz. Even the weakest prisoner would prefer silence to cringing before a German. Hochhuth disregards here the fact that the Jewish "victims" were not born as such. The majority of the *Schutzhäftlinge* came from the elite of European Jewry. They might have used their intellect for scheming and subterfuge for survival, but even the most disdainful German could never accuse them of whining and begging before him. On the other hand, the elite of the German intelligentsia was certainly not to be found in the ranks of the SS. The daemonic brilliant Doctor is miscast for this added reason.

The play would have ended logically had Pater Ricardo entered Auschwitz and fought hard to survive. Like many other priests he would have fulfilled the fundamental role of the deputy of Christ on earth, that of giving spiritual strength to all persecuted humanity, regardless of their faith. The attempt to show Ricardo's faith tempted to the breaking point by the nihilistic tauntings of the Doctor is verbosely redundant. Auschwitz itself, the well-oiled bureaucratic death factory was enough proof of the de-

---

(10) Jorge Semprun, see Chpt. I, Ftnt. 69.

structiveness of nihilism without the addition of the witty nihilistic Doctor. Volkmar Sander, in talking about the play, implies that Hochhuth lets the Doctor use Auschwitz as his personal proving ground for his hypothesis of nihilism."(11) if this is so then it is additional proof of the literary stereotyping of this figure; it would bring the stereotype closer to Mephisto than to an E.T.A. Hoffmann villain. It also emphasizes the faulty concept of the entire fifth act of the play. The existence of Auschwitz was proof that there was a whole system that disregarded the sanctity of life on which the moral judgment of the western world used to be based.

Hochhuth's accusation of organized Christianity's complicity in the Holocaust is valid. But changing the antagonist into a Faustian daemon, depicting the Jews as a whining mass of sheep being led to the slaughter, makes the play, and especially the last act, nonrealistic. It would seem that the author sacrificed truth for a dramatic structure that demanded the presentation of types. Hochhuth probably never consciously strove for dissociation as he created these characters. However, when he created Schiller-like figures and placed them into the anything but Schillerian setting of Auschwitz, the results were simply unconvincing and dissociative.

The second play on this topic to gain world renown was Peter Weiss' documentary based on the Frankfurt trials of 1963-64. *Die Ermittlung, Oratorium in 11 Gesängen(12)* was written in 1964 and first published in *Theater 1965*, a special edition of *Theater Heute, (13)* in August of 1965. In an appendix to the text

---

(11) Volkmar Sander, *Die Faszination des Bösen. Zur Wandlung des Menschenbildes* (Göttingen: Sachse und Pohl Verlag, 1968), p. 66 ff.
(12) Peter Weiss, "Die Ermittlung", in Peter Weiss Dramen 2 (Frankfurt a/M: Suhrkamp Verlag,1968), pp. 9-199.
(13) Sonderausgabe, *Theater heute* (Bad Godesberg:

81

as the main function of this theatrical form. In the same appendix, among other commentaries, Weiss poses a question that has rarely been so bluntly and precisely verbalized: "Warum wird eine historische Person, eine Periode oder Epoche aus dem Bewusstsein gestrichen?"(14)

In a structure based on Dante's *Inferno,* **Weiss'** *Ermittlung* leads the audience from the gates of Hell, the selection ramp of Auschwitz, to the center of Hell, the fiery furnaces.(15) All of the damned are condemned, not by their sins, but by the decision of a universally acknowledged government.

Unlike Hochhuth, Weiss has not attempted to fictionalize the documentary material. He merely stylized the language of the recorded court proceedings of the Frankfurt trial as they were reported in Bernd Naumann's book.(16) He has put his theories about the functions of effective documentary theater into practice, i.e., the creation of a model of the actual events out of selectively chosen fragments of reality, presentation of the facts for the appraisal of the audience, objective observation and reporting.(17) Accusers' and defendants' testimony is heard equitably on each item of the accusation. No judgment is rendered in the proceedings on the stage, it is only an inquiry. But a judgment is clearly suggested to the audience who listens to the damning testimony of the survivors and the innocuous denials of the accused in the face of the accusers' testimony. It has been said that Weiss, by limiting himself to the material

---

Friedrich Verlag, 1965), 58-87.
(14) Peter Weiss, p. 465.
(15) Henning Rischbieter, "Die Ermittlung," in *Peter Weiss* (Velben:Friedrichs Verlag,1967),p.68; ff.
(16) Bernd Naumann, *Auschwitz, Bericht über die Strafsache gegen Mulka u.a. vor dem Schwurgericht Frankfurt* (New York: F.A. Praeger, Inc.,1966).
(17) P. Weiss, p. 465 ff.

published in the Suhrkamp edition of 1968 Weiss gives his interpretation of the purposes of the documentary theater: criticism of different aspects of society is seen from the Frankfurt trial only, has failed to put Auschwitz into the context of Germany and the NS period.(18) This accusation holds true for the German past, but Weiss has established the connection to the present German development since 1945. It becomes clear in the proceedings that every one of the accused has not only gone scot-free until the time of the trial, but each one of them is in excellent financial circumstances. Several of them still work for, or receive generous pensions from, the slave labor industries they worked for in Auschwitz. Others, having worked in the camp management directly, enriched themselves through the theft of valuables from the incoming transports of victims. These accusations are put into precise words by the prosecutor in the fifth canto:(19)

> Lassen Sie es uns deutlich aussprechen
> und damit die Aussagen bestätigen
> in denen ein früherer Zeuge
> auf das System der Ausbeutung hinwies
> die für das Lager galt
> Sie Herr Zeuge
> sowie die anderen Direktoren
> der grossen Konzerne
> erreichten durch unbegrenzten Menschenverschleiss
> Jahresumsätze von mehreren Milliarden
> Lassen Sie es uns noch einmal bedenken
> dass die Nachfolger dieser Konzerne heute
> zu glanzvollen Abschlüssen kommen
> und dass sie sich wie es heisst
> in einer neuen Expansionsphase befinden(20)

---

(18) Henning Rischbieter, p. 65.
(19) P. Weiss, p. 93.
(20) P. Weiss, p. 102.

Rather than leftist propaganda, as it was designated in a review by Joel Carmichael(21), this must be understood as an expression of outrage in the name of the victims, who see the crimes against themselves and their fellow prisoners rewarded by prosperity and worldwide esteem.

Weiss has placed people of normal everyday appearance into the drab unemotional setting of a courtroom. The accused are not seen as larger-than-life, jackbooted devils; the accusers, former victims, are not seen as pitiful, emaciated, hairless spectres. The dramatis personae do not demand *a priori* sympathy for the "victims" or rejection of the "murderers." The words of the accusers' narrations are unemotional and precise, only their content is hair-raising. It seems as if Weiss did not want to detract from the dramatic content by any direction for vocal or facial expressions. There is only one kind of stage direction: repeated laughter on the part of the accused.

In *Die Ermittlung,* Weiss does not enable his audience to dissociate from the past with the help of alienating stereotypes. On the contrary, in his theories, mentioned above, he demands concrete confrontation and association of his audience with the specific period. He achieves this by stylizing selectively chosen sections of the documented testimony of accuser and accused alike. The exclusion of the word "Jew" from the entire script can be seen as an extreme attempt at emotional objectivity, since Weiss himself is a German Jew.

Even the testimony of Witness # 3 in the fourth canto, though it too might be interpreted as leftist propaganda by an unfriendly critic like Carmichael, is no more than a confirmation of observations made by Améry about the

---

(21) Joel Carmichael, "Peter Weiss' Auschwitz," in *Encounter,* XXVI, 1 Jan. 1966, 90-93.

ideologically motivated prisoner. The testimony concerns the senselessness of the suffering and death of so many victims:

> Verstört und stumm
> gingen sie den letzten Weg
> und liessen sich töten
> weil sie nicht verstanden
> Wir nennen sie Helden
> doch ihr Tod war sinnlos ....
> Es war unsere Stärke
> dass wir wussten
> warum wir hier waren
> das half uns
> unsere Identität zu bewahren.(22)

Here are Amery's observations on the same topic: "Die religiös und politisch gebundenen Kameraden waren nicht oder nur wenig erstaunt, dass im Lager das Unvorstellbare Ereignis wurde.... Sowieso war ihr Reich nicht das Hier und Heute, sondern das Morgen und das Irgendwo: das chiliastisch überstrahlte Morgen des Gläubigen oder das utopisch-irdische des Marxisten.... Prügel oder Gastod waren das erneuerte Leiden der Märtyrer oder das selbstverständliche politische Märtyrium."(23) The word *sinnlos* in Weiss' quotation is therefore not to be interpreted as "meaningless" because no resistance was offered, but as "meaningless" because of the lack of ideological conviction on the part of the victims.

It has been suggested that Weiss is so intent upon recapturing the atmosphere of horror that his writing often becomes prurient.(24) Considering the situations they describe, the words are precise-- if anything, understated.

---

(22) P. Weiss, p. 86 f.
(23) Jean Améry, p. 28 f.
(24) Jack Zipes, p. 57.

Clean, euphonious words are hard to find for a description of Auschwitz. To suggest that Weiss is "... fascinated more than any of us by the cruelty and gory bestialities ...."(25) imputes to him a sadistic mind bent on tickling a jaded audience's hunger for the sensational. Such reproach suggests the same evasion of facts that prompted earlier authors to distort NS personnages in their writings so they and the readers would not have to identify with them.

Weiss' de-emotionalized presentation of actual transcripts is far from any prurient sensationalism. If there is any distortion intended to influence the audience, other than through the words of the official documents, it was injected in a very subtle way; as mentioned previously, Weiss uses one stage direction only at certain points of the play: hearty or derisive laughter is called for from the bench of the accused whenever a facetious answer is given by one of them to a damning indictment. This stylizing by selective stage direction serves as a subliminal suggestion to the audience to take note of the callow insensitivity of the accused. Weiss also uses the pompous official terminology of the NS period in such a way that it becomes a sarcastic parody of itself, very similar to Alexander Kluge's style of language parody. A good example is the following formal phrasing in the context of an extremely cruel description by one of the former SS-men:

> Angeklagter 3 Der Zweck der Vernehmung
> war erreicht
> wenn das Blut durch die Hosen lief ...
> Sie unterlaen meiner befehlsbestimmten
> Verantwortung....(26)

---

(25) Ernst Wendt, "What is investigated?" in *German Theatre Today: A selection from the periodical 'Theater heute'* (Bad Godesberg: Friedrich Verlag, 1967), p. 39.
(26) P. Weiss, p. 71.

Weiss lets one of the SS-officers in the dock explain the source of his unquestioning obedience: the conditioned thinking to which they had submitted willingly. Without further comment from the author this testimony reveals the corruption of a whole generation of young Germans:

> Angeklagter 12 Ich möchte das einmal erklären
> Jedes dritte Wort in unserer Schulzeit
> handelte von denen
> die an allem Schuld waren
> und die ausgemerzt werden mussten
> ... und dass dies nur zum besten
> des eigenen Volkes sei.(27)

The following lines of one of the witnesses for the prosecution can be seen as the logical sequence to the above mentioned national brainwashing:

> Sie töteten nicht aus Hass und nicht aus Ueberzeugung
> sie töteten nur weil sie töten mussten
> und dies war nicht der Rede wert ... (28)

The repeated statistics of transports expedited to the gas, daily death rate and orders executed can be interpreted as a link to German history in general. The same proverbial German efficiency and discipline that made the German Empire a leading industrial nation before World War I and that propelled it again into a leading economic position after World War II, was at work in perpetrating the world's most efficient genocidal operation during the NS interim. The testimony of the accused emphasizes their satisfaction in their efficient execution of orders. They were well-disciplined executives in the camp business. Their own testimony about the important posi-

---

(27) P. Weiss, p. 119.
(28) P. Weiss, p. 74.

tions they hold in 1963 is a confirmation of their unchanged purposeful efficiency. One sentence of the prosecuting attorney deflates any assertions that these men acted under pressure:

> Es ist in keinem Fall erwiesen
> dass demjenigen der sich weigerte
> bei Tötungen mitzuwirken
> etwas geschehen wäre.(29)

Prior to writing the play, Peter Weiss participated in a guided tour of Auschwitz conducted by the German Courts. In a short story, *Meine Ortschaft,(30)* he set down his impressions of the place that might have been his place of death as it had been for so many millions. The story ends with the engimatic words: " ... es ist noch nicht zu Ende."(31) The meaning of these words becomes very clear in the light of the defense attorney's summation in *Die Ermittlung.(32)* The summation abounds with base insinuations, couched in legal jargon, about the unreliability of prejudiced witnesses for the prosecution and the "vagueness" of the sources of information. The evils of the past are not dead.

In his book *Der Totenwald(33)* Ernst Wiechert unwittingly confirms the tacit awareness of the German nation about the concentration camps in 1938, though he repeatedly denies it throughout the book. This tacit complicity of the German nation is reemphasized in the testimony of prosecution witnesses about the events since the start of the deportations.

---

(29) P. Weiss, p. 146.
(30) P. Weiss, "Meine Ortschaft," in Peter Weiss *Rapporte* (Frankfurt a/M: Suhrkamp Verlag,1968), p. 113-124.
(31) P. Weiss, *Rapporte,* p. 124.
(32) P. Weiss, p. 196.
(33) Ernst Wiechert, *Der Totenwald,* p. 70.

>   Zeuge 3
>   Ich bitte nur
>   darauf hinweisen zu dürfen
>   wie dicht der Weg von Zuschauern
>   gesäumt war
>   als man uns aus unseren Wohnungen
>   vertrieb
>   und in die Viehwagen lud ... (34)

Weiss lets the unadorned record challenge the audience to make its own judgment on crimes that had been cloaked in legality by their former government. He has created *Die Ermittlung* according to his own theories about effective documentary theater.(35) Stylizing touches can be discerned in the selection of the sections chosen from the trial documents for the strongest possible impact without digressing into the endless legal bickering attached to such proceedings. To a lesser degree, the stage directions, limited to one set of circumstances exclusively, the derisive laughter of the accused, are also used to unobtrusively influence the audience. Faced with this play, a German audience cannot help but recognize their next-door neighbors in the defendants. In German literature of the sixties dealing with concentration and extermination camps, techniques to direct the reader and/or audience toward association with the NS regime events increasingly replace methods of dissociative stereotyping.

Rolf Schneider, a young East German writer is also treating this topic with a view to forcing recognition of the past events. Like Peter Weiss, he too belongs to the group of *engagé* post-war authors. In his play *prozess*

---

(34) P. Weiss, p. 194 f.
(35) P. Weiss, p. 465 ff.

in nürnberg(36) he has carried the theme of industrial-military complicity in the events of the Holocaust a step further. His play is based on documentary material from the first and most famous war crimes trial, the Nürnberg trial of 1945-46. His sources are the 42-volume protocol of the International Military Tribunal in Nürnberg and the records of the American court psychologist G.M. Gilbert.(37) In the notes to the play Schneider elaborates on his reasons for writing the documentary. Due to the lack of electronic communications media at the time, the trial never attained the dissemination to the German public that Schneider feels it should have had. He feels that too much of it has been conveniently forgotten. He sees a growing misinterpretation of Adorno's famous dictum: "... man könne nach Auschwitz keine Gedichte mehr schreiben ... "(38) Schneider maintains "ich zweifle nicht an Adornos lauterkeit ... sehe ich mit welch beängstigender fertigkeit dieses wort kolportiert wird, scheint es mir nur hinzudeuten auf die absicht, auschwitz auch sonst nicht zu nennen: flinkes argument für eine gesellschaftliche amnesie."(39)

Schneider's style and the structure of the play are imitative of Weiss. Like Weiss he leads his audience step by step from the surface to the depths of the NS political, industrial and military hierarchy. The lowest level is the group who, in Schneider's opinion, represented the evil spirit which corrupted a whole nation to accept genocide as a justifiable aim: the hatepress. Schneider has been more successful in tying the events of the Holocaust

---

(36) Rolf Schneider, 'prozess in nürnberg," in Rolf Schneider, *Stücke* (Berlin: Henschelverlag, Kunst und Gesellschaft, 1970), pp. 113-201.
(37) R. Schneider, p. 206.
(38) R. Schneider, p. 204.
(39) R. Schneider, p. 204.

to the whole German nation and history than have other playwrights. This is partly due to the nature of the material used, since the interrogations dealt with the total personal record of each of the accused. The selective emphasis is clearly on the voluntary participation of each man before the legitimation of the regime in 1933, as can be seen from the following piece of dialogue:

>   der erste verteidiger
>   ... die stärke ihrer fraktion im
>   reichstag resultierte woraus?
>   göring
>   aus den normalen wahlen, die stattgefun-
>   den hatten:
>   auf grund des geltenden wahlgesetzes.
>   ... wir sind auf völlig legalem wege
>   zur macht gekommen. nicht anders als
>   die regierungen vorher. (40)

Schneider also refutes by documentation the repeated claim of ignorance of "unauthorized" cruelties by higher officials:

>   der amerikanische ankläger
>   die aussage von hans bernd gisevius.
>   er war 1933 beamter der gestapo.
>
>   gisevius
>   *vom tonband* in dieser neuen polizei-
>   behörde herrschten ungeheuerliche
>   zustände ... göring hatte sich diese
>   polizei als besonderes reservat vorbe-
>   halten.
>   er stellte sogenannte blankvollmächte
>   aus für morde. im verhältnis zu dem
>   was wir alle später erlebt haben war
>   das gewiss nur anfängerhaft,
>   aber so fing es an.

---

(40) R. Schneider, p. 121 f.

> göring
>> *vom tonband* ... hier habe ich keine
>> gerechtigkeit zu üben. hier habe ich
>> nur zu vernichten und auszurotten.(41)

The pre-1933 connections and enthusiastic approval of the leading industrial figures with Hitler's aspirations are disclosed in the scene *markterfordernisse II*. The scene represents the interrogation of Hjalmar Schacht, the former *Rechtsminister* for economics.

Two scenes of the play deal with the persecution and organized genocide of the Jews. The first scene, *die technik der agression*, establishes the active complicity of the German military in actions of the *Einsatzgruppen*, the Gestapo commandos in charge of liquidating Jews and Soviet political commissars in the German occupied territories of Russia. The testimony of General Keitel, that "... die wehrmacht hatte alles getan um die vom kriege betroffene zivilbevölkerung im feindgebiet zu unterstützen ... (42) is refuted by a member of an *Einsatzkommando* (Subdivision of *Einsatzgruppen*). This man gives a detailed description of the commandos' activities, including the manner of rounding up the Jews and the different kinds of executions. The direct connection between the army and the *Einsatzgruppen* is made clear in the following:

> keitel
>> das ist natürlich grauenvoll, man müsste
>> sich schämen, ein deutscher zu sein.

---

(41) R. Schneider, p. 130 f.
(42) R. Schneider, p. 153.

>   aber dies haben die ss-banditen zu
>   verantworten. die wehrmacht hatte
>   nichts damit zu tun.
>
>   der französische ankläger
>   zeuge ohlendorf: zwischen welchen
>   instanzen wurde der einsatz der
>   kommandos vereinbart?
>
>   ohlendorf
>   zwischen dem reichssicherheitshauptamt
>   und dem oberkommando der wehrmacht ...
>   die armeekommandos hatten auch zu
>   bestimmen in welcher art ... diese
>   gruppen zum einsatz gelangten.(43)

Alexander Kluge in his story *Oberleutnant Boulanger(44)* points out precisely such connections between *Einsatzgruppe* for the purpose of securing undamaged severed heads of Soviet Jewish commissars for the anthropological research project of the famous German craniologist Dr. Hirt. The story is based on an actual wartime project of Dr. Hirt, condoned and aided by the military.(45)

The second scene dealing with the Jewish persecution is the final and most extensive scene of the play: *meinungsbildungen*. Julius Streicher, the main defendant in this scene represents, in Schneider's view, the most dangerous group tried in this proceeding: the "hatepress," the mind manipulators who laid the ground rules for the Holocaust thirteen years before the *Endlösung*. As the crematoria represent the final culmination of horrors in *Die Ermittlung*, so Streicher represents the most insidious

---

(43) R. Schneider, p. 157.
(44) Alexander Kluge, *Lebensläufe*, p. 1.
(45) Raul Hilberg, The Destruction of the European Jews (Chicago: Quadrangle Books, Inc., 1961), p. 608.

evil of all the guilty groups on trial: the literary hatemongers.

In the interrogation Streicher attempts to minimize the opinion-forming power of his weekly *"Der Stürmer"* by passing it off as part of the accepted literature throughout German history: " ... anti-semitisches schrifttum hat es in deutschland gegeben durch jahrhunderte."(46) The prosecution proves conclusively, however, that *Der Stürmer* did in effect accustom the German nation, through its hate exhortations, to the acceptance of anti-Semitic cruelties culminating in organized extermination. The witness Höllriegel, ex-SS man formerly employed in the KZ Mauthausen, confirms the prosecution's claim while he discusses a particularly brutal form of torture reserved for Jewish inmates:

> höllriegel
> es sein doch saujuden gewesen, bei denen so was zugelassen war, bitte. das hat damals jeder geglaubt ... es ist uns so gesagt worden ... in den schulungsabenden bitte, in den druckschriften ...
> 'das schwarze korps,' bitte. dann haben wir noch gehabt: den 'stürmer.' (47)

Even more revealing of the mental corruption of the nation by the hatepress is the testimony of Höss, the former commandant of Auschwitz who calmly describes his part in the murder of two million men, women and children in Auschwitz. He rationalizes his unquestoning cooperation in these crimes as follows:

> höss
> ... für uns ss war das eine selbstverständlichkeit, dass die juden

---

(46) R. Schneider, p. 184.
(47) R. Schneider, p. 187.

> an allem schuld hätten ...
> wir haben doch nie etwas anderes
> gehört. wir sollten doch deutschland
> vor den juden schützen ... es ist doch
> auch in den zeitungen gestanden, wie
> dem 'stürmer.' (48)

Schneider makes it abundantly clear through the trial proceeding that not only those men were guilty who stood in the docks at Nürnberg or Frankfurt. He accuses a people who let its collective mind be so warped that extermination of a group out of their midst became acceptable because they had been conditioned to think of them as noxious vermin. Though Schneider lives and works in the DDR he does not single out any part of the divided nation as more or less guilty than the other.

Like Weiss, Schneider also lets the selected phrases of the documentaries carry the main burden of the impact. He avoids stage directions that might influence the audience against the accused as Weiss had done in *Die Ermittlung*. In one section, however, Schneider resorts to distinct stereotyping. In attempting or purporting to recreate the German speech pattern of the Russian Jew abram gerzewitsch suzkewer(49), a witness for the prosecution in the last scene, the language emerges as a persiflage of the Yiddish language as it was used by the *Stürmer* in a derogatory manner when that newspaper wanted to reproduce dialogue among Jews. This manner of speaking is derisively called *mauscheln* in German.

---

(48) R. Schneider, p. 190 f. Though Höss' name does not appear in the official list of defendants in the Nürnberg trial, he was in Nürnberg in 1946, because Kaltenbrunner's counsel had demanded him as a witness for the defense. From: Rudolf Hoess: *Commandant of Auschwitz,* transl. by Constantine FitzGibbon (London: Weidenfeld & Nicolson, Ltd., 1959), p. 174.
(49) R. Schneider, p. 181.

Schneider imposes this derogatory speech pattern not only on the rather minor figure of abram gerzewitsch suzkewer in *prozess in nürnberg,* but makes it one of the distinctive traits of the very unsavory protagonist of another one of his plays, *Die Geschichte vom Moischele(50).* This play was written between 1964 and 1965 an Schneider comments about it as follows:

> es gibt kaum ein Projekt, auf das ich so viel Mühe verwendet habe: mit dem Ergebnis, dass diese Mühe schliesslich vergeblich war. Ich hänge an diesem Stoff und weiss ... dass ich ihn niemals bewältigen werde. Ich habe ihn dennoch an die Oeffentlichkeit entlassen ... als öffentliches Bekenntnis einer unglücklichen Liebe.(51)

Schneider wanted to create an "exemplarische Erziehungsgeschichte," showing "in der Abfolge von Ver-Bildung und Bildung"(52) the controversial moralities prevalent in Germany during the past three decades. The main character, Moischele, is more anti-hero than hero. The play narrates in twelve scenes his journey from a poor Polish village through persecution, ghetto, concentration camp, to postwar racketeering and finally to a re-education camp for juvenile delinquents in the DDR. Joseph, the German anarchist whom Moischele first meets while fighting with the Jews in the ghetto rebellion, is partly his mentor, partly his nemesis. Their second confrontation occurs in the concentration camp where Joseph is *Lagerältester* and Moischele is an inmate hated by everyone for his chicanery and for his fawning upon the German camp personnel. After the war Joseph gives up a promising

---

(50) Rolf Schneider, "Die Geschichte vom Moischele" in Rolf Schneider, *Stücke,* p. 209-278.
(51) R. Schneider, "Gedanken über Theater," in R. Schneider *Stücke,* p. 345.
(52) R. Schneider, p. 345.

career to become an educator in a youth rehabilitation camp so that he may help Moischele to become a man. He will re-educate him to overcome his "ganef" tendencies, which the war and the Holocaust have brought out in him. Thus he atones on a one-to-one basis for collective German guilt.

If this fragment is the result of an unhappy love for the Jewish people, as Schneider calls it, it is a love fraught with ambiguity. What emerges in the figure of Moischele is a composite of the worst traits ascribed to the Jews by the German hatepress. Moischele, supposedly as a result of the German reign of terror, appears as a callous exploiter, catering to the weaknesses and vices of his oppressors for profit and survival. Having survived, he continues his nefarious activities by becoming a black market racketeer whose crowning *chutzpah* is the sale of an American tank. Joseph, the former anarchist, on the other hand, emerges from the war with a social conscience, ready to salvage the refuse of humanity in the person of Moischele and his like. According to Schneider, the "ganef" tendencies are only latent in a Jew. Joseph, under the same circumstances quasi-purified by the experience, emerges as a superior human being.

For the sake of local color and "authentic" dialect, Schneider lets his Jewish characters make utterances such as: "... e Goj wos schmust jiddisch, soll sein Kapore far mech...."(53) or: "Hör zu, Schlomme, wir sind beide mosaisch. Dich muss das freuen, wenn ich die Goys ein bissel beganef."(54) Perhaps Schneider's aim was to present an

---

(53) R. Schneider, p. 209.
(54) R. Schneider, p. 218.

objective, naturalistic image of the Jewish protagonist who had been represented as either noble and sad, or as helpless victim by such writers as Richter, Böll, or Andersch(55) in the past decade. This follows to a certain extent the trend of the sixties, when victims and culprits alike are treated objectively in literature. But in so doing, Schneider has gone to an extreme which borders an offensive caricature of the characters. To counterbalance the derogatory anti-Christian remarks made by the Jewish characters, Schneider also puts derogatory anti-Semitic remarks in the mouth of Joseph, the anarchist, such as: "Oh, ihr seid höflich. Ihr seid grosse Scheisser allesamt. Ihr habt noch vorm Totschlagen ein Benehmen ... so schleimig ..."(56) In Joseph the development from anti-Semitic anarchist to devoted educator of victims of Fascism is only made all the more impressive through such remarks. This man hates Nazis and Jews with equal venom at the outset of the play. His *Erziehung* to a social conscience, obviously in the socialist sense of the word, is a straight upward line, whereas Moischele's *Erziehung* takes the opposite course. The inference is clear: good human material is made firm and refined by suffering, and vice versa. It seems, however, too much of a coincidence that all weaknesses should be combined in the figure of the unsavory Jewish boy. Moischele is the opposite of Slomon, the Jewish cobbler, in Richter's *Sie fielen aus Gottes Hand.(57)* Slomon is depicted as a composite of the stereotyped noble victim. Moischele is a composite of the worst anti-Semitic clichés of the era whose victim he is supposed to be.

This manner of characterization of the victim might be seen in the context of the literary trend of objectivity of the period. However, not one of Schneider's contemporaries presents such anti-Semitic characterizations, when

---

(55) Alfred Andersch, *Sansibar oder der letzte Grund* (Olten und Freiburg i.Br.: Walter Verlag,1957).
(56) R. Schneider, 2.224.
(57) H.W. Richter, see Chapter II.

describing Jewish personnages. The suspicion arises that Schneider, in the guise of objectivity, is subtly propagating the unofficial anti-Semitism of the Soviet Union whose sphere of influence includes his residence.

Another aspect of complicity in the Holocaust events is raised in Heino Kipphardt's play *Joel Brand, Die Geschichte eines Geschäfts.(58)* Weiss and Schneider accuse the German people, its leading industrialists and its military clique. Hochhuth points the finger at world Catholicism and the Pope who failed to use his immense power on behalf of the Jewish victims. Kipphardt indicts the Allies who fought this war in the name of oppressed humanity of which the Jews were the strongest symbol. Since he lists historically incontestable sources, his indictment is convincing.(59) He does not at any time minimize the German guilt in the events. But the play is a reminder to the western world of its own hypocrisy when dealing with the Jewish tragedy.

The basis for the story is the postwar revelation of an event that took place in Hungary in 1944. The Hungarian Jewish leader Joel Brand, who believed that the lives of one million Jews could be bought from the Germans with the help of the Allies, is the idealistic protagonist of the story. He is made rudely aware of the insensitivity of the Allies to the Jewish plight during an interview with Lord Moyne, British High Commissioner of Egypt in World War II. Moyne rejects the offer of the trade of Jewish lives for trucks as a German trick to drive a wedge between the Allies. The priority of political expediency superseding the lives of one million Jews is expressed by Lord Moyne in the following callous words: "Aber ich bitte Sie Herr Brand, was mache ich in unserer Lage mit einer Million Juden? Wo soll ich sie hinbringen? Wer wird die Leute

---

(58) Heino Kipphardt, *Joel Brand, Die Geschichte eines Geschäfts,* edition suhrkamp 139 (Frankfurt a/M: Suhrkamp Verlag, 1964).
(59) H. Kipphardt, "Anmerkungen zu Joel Brand," in

nehmen?"(60) Joel Brand's answer to these quasi-rhetorical questions is the climatic indictment of the play: "Wenn der Planet keinen Platz für uns hat, dann bleibt unseren Leuten nichts anderes übrig, als ins Gas zu gehen."(61)

Kipphardt has put 3-dimensional persons on the stage. He has avoided distorting the Hungarian Jews or the Palestinian Jews either to the pitiful figures of Hochhuth's Italian Jews or to the ugly caricatures of Schneider. Each member of the *Waada*, the semi-illegal organization of the Budapest Jews, is a distinct individual. Their common bond is the deportation threat to the Hungarian Jewry, their common aim to prevent the deportation. To this end they have devised the plan for the exchange of one million Jews for anything the Germans might ask for in money or valuables. But the Germans ask for heavy trucks, and the Allies refuse to support the German war effort by delivering material for it. This is one of the major stumbling blocks of the operation. The other one, humanely more tragic, has already been elaborated upon.

Joel Brand himself is a man of such high principles that he refuses to have his wife and children brought illegally across the border to safety. There are two reasons for his strong stand, both more gentlemanly than in tune with the situation. First, he believes in the safe conduct promise given to his family by Eichmann, while he, Brand, is in Turkey, negotiating the deal. Secondly, the offer to help his family comes from a fellow Jew who is known to work for the Gestapo. Brand does not want any favors from such a man. Brand is, as Grosz, the Gestapo agent, puts it cynically "...: immer redlich. Das ist eine Tugend, die

---

Joel Brand, Die Geschichte eines Geschäfts, (Frankfurt a/M: Suhrkamp Verlag, 1964),p. 141.
(60) H. Kipphardt, p. 120.
(61) H. Kipphardt, p. 120.

sehr für Auschwitz prädestiniert."(62) Brand's belief in the success of the negotiations is based on the desperate German war situation at the time of the action (1944), and his conviction of the full cooperation of the Jewish Agency in Palestine and of the Allied Powers. His faith in the Allies is a reflection of the belief of all Jews who had remained in the German occupied territories. The breach of this faith gives the play a stronger impact, for Jewish audiences especially, than the accusations levelled by Hochhuth against the Pope. The Jewish people never counted on Papal intervention on their behalf. But they always looked to England and America as their champion. They had felt that a small part of the war was fought on their behalf, for their liberation. The disclosure of Allied callousness in the face of the smoking crematoria, as Joel Brand experienced it, destroyed this belief.

To one group of characters in the play, however, Kipphardt has given a uniform set of characteristics: to the historical figures of Eichmann, Becher and Wisliceny, as well as the other German figures. He portrays them all as jovial, garrulous and pedestrian. It can be safely assumed that Hanna Arendt's report *Eichmann in Jerusalem,(63)* had a decisive influence on this specific characterization. Stripped of his daemonic accoutrements, Eichmann emerges as the conscientious little official who is determined at any cost to execute efficiently the orders of his masters who lifted him from anonymity to power. Kipphardt has fleshed out the scientific report by Hanna Arendt on the banal murderers by dramatizing the pedestrian idiosyncrasies of Eichmann, his peers and his subordinates. For example, in scene 13 one of his henchmen gives a report on the requisitioning of 4500 Jewish apartments for the use of the German occupation troops. During the report Eichmann is asked to

---
(62) H. Kipphardt, p. 28.
(63) Hannah Arendt, see Chapter II.

reconsider the sentence imposed upon an underling, who has taken eight square meters of linoleum from one of the apartments:

> Klage
>> Ein kleines Stückchen Linoleum, sagt er, acht Quadratmeter aus einer Judenwohnung, die sowieso ...
>
> Eichmann
>> Ob acht, ob achttausend Quadratmeter, ich verlange von meinen Leuten, dass sie finanziell sauber sind.(64)

Note Eichmann's total oblivion to the irony of condemning a minor theft after ordering in the same breath the theft of 4500 apartments.

Another example of Kipphardt's elaboraton on Arendt's analysis of the SS petty bourgeois is the following: Eichmann and his cohorts delight in spouting proverbs and clichés. When Brand's wife, Hansi, is brought before Eichmann, badly beaten and bruised by his henchmen, he greets her with: "Ehret die Frauen, sie flechten und weben himmlische Rosen ins irdische Leben."(65) The Schiller quotation at the sight of the bruised woman is a touch of mordant irony. In bringing out the mediocre banality of these figures, Kipphardt prevents his audience from dissociating them from the average German petty bourgeois of before, during, or after the NS period.

Though the extermination camp *per se* never becomes visible, the play is nevertheless a drama of the Holocaust in the truest sense of the word. It illuminates one of the

---

(64) H. Kipphardt, p. 74.
(65) H. Kipphardt, p. 98.

many blunders of the free world that contributed to the final massacre of the Jews in the camps. Kipphardt has produced a concrete example of the historical fact that political expediency supersedes human lives. Like Hochhuth, Kipphardt could also be accused of an attempt to alleviate the German guilt by revealing the simplicity of the free world in the *Endlösung* for political reasons. But Hochhuth's leading German figures are disguised in such theatrical stereotypes that neither readers nor audience are forced to confront their post in them. Kipphardt does not allow his German audience this comfort.

Kipphardt's work, like Weiss' and Schneider's to some extent, is representative of the German literary treatment of the NS era in general and the Holocaust period specifically after 1963. The majority of the sixties shun any evasive or stereotyped treatment. They demand of themselves and of their readers the utmost in truth and objectivity.

The preceding plays were limited by their documentary nature to treat the Holocaust within its chronological period or from the perspective of the trial setting. Nelly Sachs' mystery play *Eli, Ein Mysterienspiel vom Leiden Israels,(66)* written in 1943 (first produced in Germany as a radio play in 1961), was able to transcend the time and place of the Holocaust. *Eli* is a product of both German and Jewish culture. It stands in the tradition of German Romanticism as well as Chassidic folklore. The time of the play is designated as *Nach dem Martyrium,(67)* a nebulous concept in 1943. Setting

---

(66) Nelly Sachs, "Eli, Ein Mysterienspiel vom Leiden Israels," in Nelly Sachs, *Das Leiden Israels* (Frankfurt a/M: Suhrkamp Verlag, 1965), pp. 7-67, first published, private edition, Malmö, 1951.
(67) Nelly Sachs, p. 6.

the play into a future that could only be dimly discerned at that time adds to its fairy tale quality. Its creation thereby also affirms Nelly Sachs' belief in a heavenly mercy that would grant survival and a future to the remnants of Israel.

Throughout the play Nelly Sachs reaffirms the need of the Jewish people to live and rebuild in spite of the Holocaust, or perhaps because of it. She thus dramatizes in 1943 a concept that has been expressed as late as 1972 by the Jewish philosopher Emil L. Fackenheim as the philosophical axiom for Judaism after Auschwitz: "The imperative is to hand Hitler no posthumous victory. It is a positive command to survive as a people and remember the victims. It is a prohibition against despair of man and his world, lest the world be handed over to the forces of Auschwitz."(68) Though Nelly Sachs produced her major literary works in exile, she never lost contact with the German literary tradition in which she had grown up. Hilde Domin acknowledges Nelly Sachs as a German writer in the following tribute: " ... und [Du] bist daher ein deutscher Dichter und kannst gar nicht anders sein .... Da wird einer verstossen, verfolgt ... und in der Verzweiflung ergreift er das Wort und erneut es ... das Wort, das zugleich das Seine ist und das der Verfolger."(69)

Like Schneider's *Die Geschichte vom Moischele,* Sachs' play also deals with the Polish Jews, but her stylizing of the Yiddish inflection does not have the parodistic quality that is so offensive in Schneider's work. Her language is more reminiscent of the translations of folk tales by Sholem Alechem and Shalom Asch. She uses

---

(68) Michael A. Meyer, "The Religious Thought of Emil L. Fackenheim, Judaism after Auschwitz," in *Commentary,* LIII, 6, June 1972, 55-62.
(69) Hilde Domin, "Offener Brief an Nelly Sachs," in *Nelly Sachs zu Ehren,* ed. Walter A. Berendson (Frankfurt a/M: Suhrkamp Verlag, 1966).

the language of the Jewish legends to create a twentieth century legend of the suffering of Israel. The following is one of the many examples of her sensitive stylizing of the Yiddisch inflection:

> Weine nicht Jossele,
> Bauen wir doch aufs neue das alte Haus.
> Hängen sich die Tränen ans Gestein,
> hängen sich die Seufzer ans Gebälk,
> können nicht schlafen die kleinen Kinder,
> hat der Tod ein weiches Bett.(70)

She is " ... bedacht das Unsägliche auf eine transzendente Ebene zu ziehen, um es aushaltbar zu machen."(71) Compared with such lyric stylizing of the jargon, Schneider's ... a Goj was schmust jiddisch ... etc.(72) appears all the more as crass persiflage.

A small Polish country town, predominantly Jewish before the war, is the scene to which the survivors of the Holocaust have returned to rebuild their lives and their homes. Prior to the action of the play the child Eli had been brutally murdered by a soldier during a Sonderaktion. Eli had sounded his shepherds pipe to the heavens as if appealing for help and the soldier had seen this action as a signal of attack against him. Among the returned Jews is Michael the cobbler, one of the thirty-six Just Men of Chassidic folklore. Michael fulfills the task assigned by God to the Just, that of taking the sorrows of his fellow Jews on himself so that they may be free to rebuild their lives. Michael's power to mend the souls of his people is paralleled in his occupation as a cobbler who sews the

---
(70) Nelly Sachs, p. 14.
(71) Siegfried Melchinger, "Anmerkungen zu den Spielen," in *Nelly Sachs zu Ehren,* ibid p. 162.
(72) R. Schneider, p. 209.

lowers of the shoes to the uppers in an analogy of rejoining body and soul. For this reason shoes in his hands have a magical property. They call forth images and voices from the past. While he handles the shoes of the murdered child Eli, Michael bears the ghostly sounds of Eli's shepherd's pipe. He is thereby launched on his quest for the child's murderer. On his long journey to the land of the former enemy (Sachs never uses the word "German" throughout the whole play), Michael passes through a world of dreams and unearthly appearances. In the village beyond the border where Michael seeks work as a cobbler, the sounds of Eli's pipe, as he plays it, delight the innocent, children and young animals alike. The adult men of the village cannt bear the sound of it. God's voice in the pipe is music to the innocent but terror to the guilty. When one of the villagers brings his shoes to be repaired, Michael's magic powers let him recognize the murderer in the shoes. At the same time every man in the village who carries a burden of guilt from the Holocaust is haunted by unearthly incidents recalling their deeds. The Just Man's powers are strong enough to force the murderers to confession of their guilt. In the final scene Eli's murderer is annihilated by the wrath of God, and Michael, whose task is fulfilled ("Deine Schuhe sind vertreten - komm.")(73) is carried off to heaven.

The structure of the *Stationendrama* can be found in German literature in the medieval mystery plays and in the expressionist dramas such as Georg Kaiser's *Von Morgens bis Mitternacht(74)*. Considering that Nelly Sachs herself calls the play specifically *Ein Mysterienspiel*, the medieval model seems more likely. Like so many Romantics, Nelly Sachs has created a new folktale. The

---

(73) Nelly Sachs, p. 67.
(74) Georg Kaiser, "Von Morgens bis Mitternacht; Stück in zwei Teilen," in *Georg Kaiser, Werke*, ed. Walter Huder (Berlin: Propyläen Verlag, 1970), Vol. I.

basis of this folktale, the Holocaust, is thereby transposed from the suffering and guilt of mortals to a level where victims and executioners alike become archetypical models of human traits. Nelly Sachs' *Eli* has been included here for the reason that it belongs to the few existing plays with the Holocaust as its main topic. Being neither stylized documentary nor the dramatization of an actual specific occurrence, its message of Good, Evil and Divine Justice lies on a universal level, and has timeless validity. Analysis as to stereotyping or stylizing is therefore not applicable to this quasi-folktale play.

The German dramas about the Holocaust treated in this chapter reflect the matured attitude of the sixties toward the topic. With the exception of Nelly Sachs' *Eli,* for the reasons listed above, and Rolf Hochhuth's *Der Stellvertreter,* all the plays aim at demythologizing the NS regime and its participants. The traits of mediocrity and *Spiessbürgerlichkeit* in the characterizations of the Nazi are heightened either through stylizing or caricature. By these theatrical techniques the uninterrupted reign of the efficient German bureaucrats, businessmen and officer corps from before 1933 through the Holocaust period and into the postwar era has to be acknowledged by the audience.

Rolf Hochhuth's *Stellvertreter* does not yet reflect this objectivity; his personages are Schillerian types in a Schillerian drama. The larger-than-life characterizations do not demand identification with the actual persons they represent, because of their dramatic size. Hochhuth took the living models for his characters out of the context of reality when he draped the mantle of Schillerian grandeur on them. His dramatis personae result in dissociative stereotyping.

CHAPTER IV

POSTWAR GERMAN LITERATURE ABOUT THE PERIOD
PRIOR TO THE HOLOCAUST AND
AFTER THE HOLOCAUST

The actual Holocaust was not a phenomenon that sprang fullfledged from the foreheads of its creators. The shadow of these things to come lay over Germany throughout the entire period of the NS Regime. Jean Améry recalls his moment of shocked awareness about his threatened existence as a Jew:

> Es fing ... an, als ich 1935 in einem Wiener Cafe über einer Zeitung sass und die eben drüben in Deutschland erlassenen Nürnberger Gesetze studierte .... Die Gesellschaft, sinnfällig im nationalsozialistischen deutschen Staat, den ... die Welt als legitimen Vertreter des deutschen Volkes anerkannte, hatte ... meinem ... Wissen, dass ich ein Jude sei, eine neue Dimension gegeben.... Wenn das von der Gesellschaft über mich verhängte Urteil einen greifbaren Sinn hatte, konnte es nur bedeuten, ich sei fürderhin dem Tode ausgesetzt.... Es war ... kein revolutionärer Radau, sondern die in einem Slogan-- Kriegsruf!-- verdichtete wohldurchdachte Forderung eines Volkes.(1)

Martin Buber says of the even more threatening event of the *Kristallnacht,* the anti-Semitic riots organized

---
(1) *Jenseits von Schuld und Sühne* (München: Szczesny Verlag, 1966), p. 135f.

by the Nazis on November 9 and 10, 1938: "What happened in Germany ... was not an outbreak of a nation's passion of widespread Jew hatred.... It was a command from the upper level and was executed with the precision of a dependable machine."(2)

The events of the Holocaust throw their shadow equally over the postwar era in Germany not only in the spectacular public trials, but in the lives of victims and executioners, both of whom try to rebuild their lives. The latter attempt to hide the past, the former try to overcome it. Both these groups have been treated to some extent by postwar German writers. The amount and manner of stereotyping in the literary treatment of this period will be investigated in this chapter.

Der Ausflug der toten Mädchen,(3) the title story of a collection of short stories written by Anna Seghers in Mexican exile in 1943, recalls not only the behavior of the average German during the immediate pre-Holocaust era, but also shows the continuity and interrelation of NS Germany with its past during the early twentieth century.

Anna Seghers has created a story spanning a period from before World War I in Germany to a sunburnt courtyard in Mexico during World War II: "Daraus ergibt sich ein eigentümlicher Parallelismus der Erzählung, eine Art Pendelbewegung: zwischen der Zeit des Ersten und der des Zweiten Weltkrieges, zwischen Rückblende und Antizipation, Traum und Wachsein."(4) Recuperating from a severe ill-

---
(2) E.Wm. Rollins & Harry Zohn, *Men of Dialogue: Martin Buber, and Albrecht Goes* (New York: Funk and Wagnall, 1969), p. 237.
(3) New York: Aurora Verlag, 1946, p. 5.
(4) Marcel Reich-Ranicki, "Die kommunistische Erzählerin Anna Seghers," in *Deutsche Literatur im West und Ost* (München: R. Piper & Co., 1966), p. 377.

ness and weakened by it, the narrator experiences a daydream of overpowering reality in the middle of the Mexican landscape. She feels herself transported in time and place, back to a school excursion in the Rhine valley before the First World War. But the line between dream and reality, between past and present, is so fine that during the mirage she recalls also the fate of all her school friends as it developed immediately before and during the Hitler era. As in *Das siebte Kreuz*, the landscape of Seghers' native region, the Rhine valley around Mainz, is the only stable variant in the story. The glowing and tender description of the landscape is a reiteration of the exile's homesickness:

> .... Je mehr und je länger ich mich umsah, desto rascher füllte sich mein Herz mit Heiterkeit.... Bei dem blossen Anblick des weichen hügeligen Landes gedieh die Lebensfreude und Heiterkeit statt der Schwermut aus dem Blut selbst, wie ein bestimmtes Korn aus einer bestimmten Erde.(5)

She is attempting to reassert her claim, as in *Das siebte Kreuz*, that under normal circumstances, i.e., before the Nazi era, there was no anti-Semitism among the German people. The group of boys and girls on this excursion before World War I stands at the threshold of life as friends with equal backgrounds and equal promises for the future. Only as the projection into that future opens up do we learn that some of them will be persecuted for being Jews, some of them will perish as enemies of the NS Regime in concentration camps. The rest of the group, having prospered through the regime, will perish in the fires of the war. The class flirt will turn into the whore with the golden heart who commits suicide because her Jewish

---

(5) Anna Seghers, *Der Ausflug der toten Mädchen* (N.Y. Aurora Verlag, 1946), p. 13.

lover has been murdered. The class beauty will turn into a Nazi harridan who denounces her best friend as a socialist and thereby causes her death. Seghers mirrors in the fate of the little people the momentous historical events. She demonstrates:

> ... dass die Schicksale der Knaben und Mädchen zusammen das Schicksal der Heimat, das Schicksal des Volkes ausmachen ... (6)

In this short story Seghers also sees the people of her region as she wants to remember them. For the most part they are, in her memory, people who love their fellowmen. Most of her comrades do not change under the pressure of the NS era. They perish under persecution or remain uninvolved in the events. For those fellow students who do become ardent Nazis, Seghers always finds a rationale. There is either a great disappointment or the loss of a loved one in the war that contributes to their opting for the Nazi ideology. But innocent or guilty, whether by their own hand, through violence, or by bombs, all her classmates find death as a consequence of the Third Reich era. Only the narrator is alive to record the events for posterity. Perhaps Seghers saw a kind of poetic justice in the fact that one of the persecuted ones, the one forcefully torn from the beloved homeland, should be the only one to survive to write the story of the class of 1913.

Seghers' stereotyping of her characters is caused by nostalgia and homesickness. The antagonist of the story is the Third Reich. The women in the story become its victims, either through participation or resistance. The narrator emphasizes over and over again that in none of these women was there any predilection to cruelty and evil. She underlines the fact that the favorite teacher of

---

(6) Anna Seghers, p. 21.

the whole class, the whole school, was Fräulein Sichel, a Jewess. Seghers recognizes the Nazi era only as an aberration of a basically kind and decent people.

Albrecht Goes's story, "Das Brandopfer,"(7) is set in the postwar era. Like Seghers' story, it too, is told partly in flashbacks. But Goes has applied the stylistic means of several points of view. The narrator's tale becomes the frame for the flashbacks and a letter, each of them narrated by a different speaker. They form the body of the short story. The narrator of the frame is a librarian who rents a room in the house of the butcher Walker after the war. When renting the room from Frau Walker, he is struck not only by her atypical appearance: "Dass ihre Hände nicht für das Metzgermesser geschaffen sind, sieht jeder, und wofür die grossen dunklen Augen bestimmt sind, das frage du"(8) but also by the appearance of the rented room, obviously furnished by her, whose elegant simplicity was totally out of tune with the expectations of a room rented from a butcher. His interest in Frau Walker increases when he learns that the house he lives in is known as the *Judenmetzig,* the Jew Butchershop. He becomes more closely acquainted with her at a meeting of the *Pro Israel Gesellschaft,* a group of Germans promoting the reestablishment of dialogue between Israel and Germany. Here begins the main body of the story. Frau Walker relates to the narrator the story of the incident that brought the frightful burn to her face.

Her narration takes the reader back to the period immediately preceding the beginning of the Holocaust when anti-Jewish measures intensified and finally culminated in the *Endlösung*. The use of stores, park benches, and restaurants had already been forbidden to Jews. The Walker butcher shop had been designated by the

---
(7) Albrecht Goes, *Das Brandopfer* (Frankfurt a/M: S. Fischer Verlag, 1954).
(8) Albrecht Goes, p. 19.

authorities as one of the few shops open to Jews, and that only for a few hours each week. Thus it became the *Judenmetzig*. Every Friday afternoon the Jews were allowed to come to the shop with their ration cards marked with the letter *J*, "ein freches J,"(9) to collect their meager rations. Frau Walker observes these people, watches their number diminish by emigration or, mostly, by suicide. Then comes the period of the deportations. When a pregnant young women brings her a baby carriage and a few baby clothes, for which she will have no further use, Frau Walker is overwhelmed by the guilt of her own people. She feels that only by sacrificing herself can she cleanse all her guilty countrymen by proxy. She sets fire to her house and remains in the fire. But she is miraculously saved by a Jew, the third narrator, who that night during an air raid had been denied entrance into an air raid shelter, and who roamed the streets in search of safety. The identity of the third narrator is revealed when Frau Walker recognizes the girlfriend of the narrator-librarian after the war as the daughter of her rescuer. A letter from that man narrates his story of the night of Frau Walker's fiery suicide attempt. Frau Walker takes her rescue as a sign from God that he has not accepted her offering, because: " ... der eine, der hier aufrechnen könnte, der wird sagen, dass ihm solche Opfer nicht gefallen, dass er nicht 'Lust hat am Brandopfer' und am 'Fett von den Gemästeten,"sondern am geängsteten Geist und am zerschlagenen Herzen ... dass sie alle ... bewahrt sind zu anderem Dienste."(10) The short story found world-wide acclaim. Richard Thieberger says of it: "... la bouchere des Juifs de 'la flamme du sacrifice' pose [ent] [des] cas de conscience vu[s] par beaucoup d'Allemands, mais que peu d'écrivains seraient capables de présenter avec autant de tact, de sincérité et de force."(11)

---

(9) Albrecht Goes, p. 15.
(10) Albrecht Goes, p. 74.
(11) Richard Thieberger, "Albrecht Goes," in *Les langues modernes,* LII, 2 (mars-avril, 1958), 47-49.

Goes does not merely paint evil SS executioners and pathetic victims. He indicates through the mouth of the protagonist, Frau Walker, the degrees of anti-Semitic corruption present in the entire population: "... es gab nicht wenige, denen die Verordnung nicht gefiel und die verlegen vor sich hin schwiegen, wenn andere redeten. Aber ... rief dann einer--einer oder eine, ich weiss es nicht mehr-: Machen Sie nur freitags nacht gut Durchzug, sonst hälts kein Christenmensch bei Ihnen aus, Frau Walker."(12) or in the words of the letter writer: "So aber trug ich den Mantel und am Mantel den Stern: der Luftschutzwart im Sammelbunker entdeckte ihn auf den ersten Blick, gleich unter der Tür--und er verwehrte mir den Zutritt."(13) The casual acceptance of evil by a whole population is emphasized by the contrasting figure of Frau Walker, the almost mysterious protagonist of the story. Goes seems to have created her this way in order to underline her exceptional status among her countrymen.

As a literary figure she appears to be a direct descendant of the grandmother in Brentano's *Geschichte vom braven Kasperl und dem schönen Annerl.* Her language has the severe simplicity of the Luther bible, a language familiar to Albrecht Goes, the pastor. Like Brentano's grandmother, with no connection to her surroundings, she is linked to God by her conscience and her compassion. There are also other traits that link this story with Brentano's story as well. Goes has also included a certain amount of *deus ex machina* similar to Brentano's linking the several characters. Sabine Berendson, the narrator's girlfriend, happens to be the daughter of the Jewish man who saved Frau Walker "zu anderen Diensten."(14) The narrator has an uncanny presentiment about receiving the letter from Frau Walker which tells a part

---

(12) Albrecht Goes, p. 13.
(13) Albrecht Goes, p. 68.
(14) Albrecht Goes, p. 74.

of her story. Traditional literary stereotyping in characterization and stylistic means are successfully used by Albrecht Goes to present an unpalatable fact to the German readers in 1954: namely that the truly compassionate German was the rare exception in a nation with many shades of guilt.

Alfred Andersch's novel *Sansibar oder der letzte Grund,*(15) published in 1957, has as its setting the period preceding the Holocaust. The regime is still in the process of eliminating ideological dissenters and is only just beginning the *Endlösung* by expropriating all Jewish property in Germany. Andersch's novel tells the story of three men who are firmly grounded in their respective ideologies: the Church and the Communist Party. At this point in time they are forced to exercise their free will, to commit themselves according to their consciences. Pastor Helander, the protector of the sculpture *Reading Friar,"* created by an outlawed artist, has been trained to follow the commands of the Church. Knudsen, a middle-aged fisherman in Rerik, the Baltic village where Helander is Pastor, had been a Communist Party member like most of the fishermen of his generation. The seeming capitulation of the Party before the "others," the NS regime, has disillusioned him. But his disillusionment has not made him turn to the new regime as the other fishermen have done. He keeps to himself: "Man musste übrig bleiben, darauf kam es an."(16) Gregor, a Russian-trained Communist Party fuctionary, still does the courier work for the party. He has however begun to think for himself, a heresy for a loyal Party member, and therefore has decided to desert both the Party and his homeland, which is ruled by the "others" who persecute him.

---

(15) Alfred Andersch, *Sansibar oder der letzte Grund* (Olten & Freiburg im Breisgau: Walter Verlag, 1957).

(16) Alfred Andersch, p. 62.

Very much like Hans Werner Richter in *Sie fielen aus Gottes Hand,* Andersch also lets the lives of his protagonists converge. But since Andersch's novel takes place within a twenty-four hour period, the fates of the men, unlike those in Richter's novel, intermesh almost immediately. Pastor Helander has been informed that he will have to surrender the statue of the *Reading Friar* to the NS authorities since it is considered a piece of decadent art. He knows that the true reason for this order is the provocative impression of the sculpture: the impression of a man who acts independently and thinks independently, a heresy in the eyes of the "others," as it is a heresy in the eyes of the Communist Party. This is the tie between Pastor Helander and Gregor the defector, who sees the small work of art as the personification of his point of view. Both Gregor and Pastor Helander need Knudsen to realize their plans: escape for the statue and for the defector. Knudsen, disillusioned with the Party, hating the "others," and with no love for organized religion, feels pressured by all these negative emotions. He is asked to involve himself by men who feel as he does but are willing to commit themselves to action according to their thoughts. He resents and envies both men the ability to commit themselves to danger according to their conviction whereas he has chosen the path of least resistance for the sake of his own and his wife's survival.

A third endangered specimen is added to the list of fugitives: a young Jewess, Judith: "... ein junges schwarzhaariges Mädchen ... das einen hellen Trenchcoat anhatte, mit einem schönen zarten fremdartigen Rassengesicht ... über einem hellen eleganten Trenchcoat."(17) Gregor picks her up as she is being thrown out of the local inn. She has been trying to find a steamer for illegal passage to Sweden. Her mother has just committed suicide in the elegant family villa in Hamburg after sending

---

(17) Alfred Andersch, p. 83.

the girl off to escape. To Gregor, Judith belongs to the same group of endangered species as the statue who unlike him, have not the free choice of leaving the land of the "others," but must flee for their lives because they cannot hide the traits that endanger them. He therefore sacrifices his place in Knudsen's boat and allows the *Reading Friar,* the symbol of persecuted freedom of thought, and Judith, the symbol of racially persecuted humanity, to gain freedom. He will take the more dangerous land route out of the country to gain his freedom.

Each of the three men has exercised his will in defiance of his ingrained ideology. Helander pays for his act of defiance against the orders of his superior. When the "others" come to fetch the figure, he greets them with his gun and thereby brings about his murder. Knudsen has abandoned his passive existence, thereby jeopardizing the last safe Party link, himself, in Rerik. Gregor has broken with the Party entirely, abandoned his ideology completely. These three protagonists, and also the parabolically involved cabin boy on Knudsen's boat (for whom the final reason for flight, "der letzte Grund," is the magical island of Sansibar) are multifaceted characters. Each one of the four is motivated in the final analysis by his sense of commitment either to another human being, to an idea, or to humanity in general.

Only one figure emerges as strongly stereotyped and one-dimensional: Judith, the Jewess. Similar to Heinrich Böll's Ilona, she is the strongly philosemitic stereotype of the beautiful, exotic Jewess persecuted by cruel fate. In Judith's case, she is brought overnight from the status of well-bred young lady of good family to the status of streetwalker: "Gestern noch mit Mama in unserer Hamburger Villa, das Frühstücksporzellan und die späten Georginen und heute schon die Sprache einer Dirne."(18) It becomes clear that Judith is only an added object to drive

---

(18) Alfred Andersch, p. 103.

the plot forward. The statue of the Friar lacks emotional appeal, the addition of the beautiful exotic Jewess adds not only the philosemitic touch but also a hint of a romantic involvement which influences Gregor's decision through emotional entanglement. Judith is described as "... eines jener jungen jüdischen Gesichter, wie er sie im Jugendverband in Berlin, in Moskau, oft gesehen hatte."(19) She is Jewish, beautiful, exotic, with no other distinguishing marks. The wooden sculpture of the *Reading Friar* emerges with more dimensions than the living girl.

Wolfdietrich Schnurre, a writer of the same generation as Alfred Andersch and Heinrich Böll, has managed to treat the Jew in his short story *Freundschaft mit Adam (20)* neither with philosemitic exaggeration nor with condescending pity for the stereotyped victim. In the foreword to one of his books, Schnurre gives as the compelling reason for his writing: "Man schrieb aus Erschütterung, aus Empörung ... Man schrieb, um zu warnen."(21) And that is exactly how he writes, terse and precise and with detailed observation. The impact of this short story is not so much in his prose as in the situation he describes with the help of his words.

The story tells of the friendship of Bruno, the son of a German laborer in a small town, with Adam, the deaf and dumb retarded son of a Jewish watchmaker. Prior to the Holocaust Adam is locked up in a Jewish insane asylum in Bruno's neighborhood. The asylum is repeatedly threatened by SA and SS raids and finally all inmates are deported for extermination. With a few sentences Schnurre

---

(19) Alfred Andersch, p. 78.
(20) Wolfdietrich Schnurre, in *Eine Rechnung, die nicht aufgeht* (München: List Verlag, 1964), pp. 32-47.
(21) Wolfdietrich Schnurre, *Man sollte dagegen sein* (Olten & Freiburg im Breisgau: Walter Verlag, 1960).

sketches in the background of both Adam and Bruno. The description of Bruno's father compresses in one phrase the reason for the wholesale conversion of the German labor population to Nazism:

> ... er war lange arbeitslos gewesen und erst vierunddreissig hatte er wieder Arbeit bekommen;
> ... und jetzt las er auch nicht mehr den 'Vorwärts'
> sondern den 'Völkischen Beobachter.' (22)

The child Bruno feels compassionately attracted to the retarded Adam, a child in a man's body. He saves the few pennies he earns by selling the alarm clocks which Adam throws to him from the window of the asylum. Adam's father has given them to his son, hoping to arouse his interest in something. With the saved money, Bruno buys a toy that he knows will please Adam much more, a child's toy, a shiny green ball with gold stripes. His greatest happiness comes on the day when he can give Adam the ball personally and coax a happy smile from the frozen face. But this is also the day and the moment when the black trucks with the SS come to take the whole asylum to be exterminated. Bruno, though he knows what the trucks mean, as does everyone in the city, "Sie fuhren langsam und holpernd die ... Wörthstrasse hinauf ... Ueberall blieben die Leute stehen und sahen ihnen nach; nicht *ein* Gesicht war bestürzt,"(23) insists on staying with Adam and climbs into the truck with him.

Schnurre weaves the burgeoning friendship between the German child and the Jewish retarded man in between the matter-of-fact description of Jewish persecution, German indifference and the Nazi excesses. The juxtaposition of

---

(22) Wolfdietrich Schnurre, p. 35.
(23) Wolfdietrich Schnurre, p. 46.

the general anti-Semitism that does not stop at hating and destroying even the sick, and the bond of friendship between the German child and the Jewish man emphasizes the point of the story without further elaboration. The child does not think in terms of Jew and German. For him Adam (which means "Man" in Hebrew) is a human being who reaches out to him. Joining Adam on the truck is not an elaborate gesture of protest, like Father Ricardo's:(24) Adam's need for him and his need to protect Adam is his only consideration: " ... die Angst, er könnte doch noch von Adam getrennt werden."(25) Without philosemitic sentimentality or stereotyping, Schnurre has given an example, in the action of a child, of what German action should have been.

Like the pre-Holocaust period, so the post-Holocaust and post-war period in Germany has also become a topic of interest for several well-known postwar German writers. Their works deal with the postwar adjustment of both victims and persecutors to a normal world. It becomes obvious that the writers found much less difficulty in creating the physical settings for these stories, since they did not have to deal with locations which they never knew. The models for the characters from either category could be found in everyday life of postwar Germany. Only the psychological aspects of these characters are the creation of the writers' observation and insight.

Walter Jens's novel *Der Blinde*(26) is a case in point. The novel concerns a German teacher in postwar Germany who loses his sight through illness. His friend Moses

---

(24) Rolf Hochhuth, *Der Stellvertreter*.
(25) Wolfdietrich Schnurre, p. 46.
(26) Walter Jens, *Der Blinde* (München:R. Piper & Co., 1964). (First German publication, Rowohlt, 1960. Originally published in English, translated by Michael Bullock, London: André Deutsch, Ltd., 1954).

Matthäus, a Jewish actor who had returned from a concentration camp with all his faculties intact, has given him a set of forty-eight little blocks he had brought out of the camp to occupy the blind man physically during the first shocking period of blindness. With the help of these blocks, arranging and rearranging them on a tray, the blind Heinrich Mittenhaufen recreates locations and situations of his past life with his family. When Matthäus sees how Mittenhaufen uses the blocks to retreat into the world of the past, he explains to him the origin and the rules of the "game" for which the blocks were used in the camp. The blocks, originally carved by one of the prisoners for his grandchild in another camp, became the means of emotional and mental survival for Moses and his friends. The blocks could represent everything, houses, gardens, men, or time: "Dann begann Isaac mit den Steinen zu spielen, führte Menschen zusammen und liess sie sich trennen ... schuf Jahre, Länder und Meere und machte aus allem wieder neue Geschichten."(27) But the rules had to be observed. They were: "... man darf nur spielen, wenn man anders nicht mehr leben kann; die zweite heisst: man darf nur spielen, um Hoffnung zu schöpfen, einmal wieder leben zu können; die dritte heisst: man darf nur spielen, was in der Zukunft liegt und was man einmal glaubt verwirklichen zu können."(28) Sticking to these conditions and playing the game for the sake of their sanity helped the group of inmates to keep their will to live. Those that died did so from disease or torture, not from giving up the will to live. The seven that did survive emerged to freedom with their minds intact and capable of coping with a world they had visualized during their imprisonment. But Mittenhaufen seems incapable of playing the game according to these rules. He does not seem to have enough inner resources to play games that represent the future. He is despairing of ever again becom-

---

(27) Walter Jens, p. 52.
(28) Walter Jens, p. 54.

ing a part of his family's life and refuses to use the blocks. At this time Moses Matthäus remembers the fourth condition of the game. To illustrate the importance of this condition and of the continuing use of the game to Mittenhaufen, Moses takes him to see another survivor of his group, a man blind from birth. This man gives Mittenhaufen a second set of blocks and explains to him the all-important fourth rule: "Man darf das Spiel nicht allein spielen, denn sonst ist man verloren ... vielleicht hat jeder zuletzt für sich selbst gespielt, aber zuerst immer für den, der am gefährdesten war.... Die Steine meines Kastens, das waren für mich die Gesichter der Freunde .... Es müssen immer zwei sein; Du und der Andere."(29)

The story does not look at the past with either guilt or apology. It dwells on friendship and cooperation for survival under danger. On a deeper level it is a tale of reconcilation, erasing old gulfs of hate. The experience of two Jewish survivors of the Holocaust, which had been instigated by Heinrich Mittenhaufen's compatriots, aids him to find his way back to life. When Jens does attempt descriptions of camp conditions, a certain amount of stereotyping through ignorance of the situation becomes obvious. For instance, no blind Jew would have survived an extermination camp; only in Theresienstadt could such a man have entered alive, and even in Theresienstadt his survival was precarious. Since Matthäus mentions swamps in connection with the camp, he could not have been describing Theresienstadt, as there are no swamps near Theresienstadt. There is also talk of a *Kinderlager (30)* where the old man's grandchild lived for whom the blocks were originally destined. Again there was no children's camp in the vicinity of the extermination camps. But since these few descriptions serve only as points of departure for the story, the inaccuracies do not detract from

---
(29) Walter Jens, p. 98.
(30) Walter Jens, p. 51.

it. Its impact lies in the uniqueness of a positive application of a lesson learned under the most negative circumstances. It is interesting to note that the premise of the short story, the game, duplicates the premise of Stefan Zweig's *Schachnovelle.(31)* In both cases a game is played for sanity and survival. In Zweig's short story it is the sanity of one man, in Jens's the survival of a whole group.

Wolfgang Weyrauch's short story *Mit dem Kopf durch die Wand(32)* dealing with a survivor in postwar Germany is diametrically opposed to Jens's novel. Where Jens sees hope and reconciliation between Jewish survivors and the nation that persecuted them, Weyrauch, through the eyes of his character, sees only continued hate and oppression. The protagonist of the story is a woman whose mind has been unhinged by her experiences in the extermination camp. She still imagines herself persecuted in devious ways by the population of postwar Germany, a people that hides its undiminished anti-Semitism under politeness and indifference. The story is written in the form of a continuous inner monologue, using the expressionistic style popular in the twenties.

In the mind of the protagonist the past is not finished; it intrudes on the present and she feels continuously hunted. Much as during the Holocaust era she sees herself "... verfolgt, ohne angreifen zu dürfen,"(33) which is the most unbearable adjunct to persecution by governmental decree. But in her deranged mind this decree has become a way of life for the population of postwar Germany. She believes the children to be infected by this vicious

---

(31) Stefan Zweig, *Schachnovelle* (Frankfurt a/M: Fischer Verlag, 1957.)
(32) Wolfgang Weyrauch, *Mein Schiff, das heisst Taifun,* (Olten and Freiburg: Walter Verlag, 1959), pp. 19-31.
(33) Wolfgang Weyrauch, p. 20.

disease: "Die Kinder werden dasselbe tun, was ihre Eltern getan haben."(34) She also believes that her nearsightedness, aggravated by camp deprivations, has given her the special gift of seeing beyond the exterior of the people around her: "Ich sah die Kainszeichen ... Aber das Böse in den Augen der Fussgänger war ein anderes Böses, als man es anderswo sieht. Es war das Böse, wie ich es aus den Lagern kenne. Es war das Mörderische verborgen unter Gleichgültigkeit, gespielter Gleichgültigkeit, Höflichkeit ... verborgen, fast verborgen, kaum verborgen, aber das Mörderische."(35) The sequence goes on to a remembrance of the mass executions and the graves. Here Weyrauch expresses through the mouth of a mad woman a thought that several years later was paraphrased in Peter Weiss's play, *Die Ermittlung.*(36) She recalls her fellow Jews sentenced to death by the same people that she meets in the street at present: " ... jetzt mussten sie die Gräber, worin sie standen, selbst zuschaufeln, nicht ganz, denn das konnten sie nicht ... so dass die, welche sie zum Tode verurteilt hatten ... Hand anlegten, um die Ermordeten unsichtbar zu machen, nicht den Mord, denn für sie war es kein Mord ... sondern eine Selbstverständlichkeit."(37) Weyrauch is very much aware of the hypocrisy of the successful German businessman with a guilty past: "Natürlich kommt es auf den Inhalt meiner Fragen an. Er ist unbequem ... Er beschäftigt sich mit einer Vergangenheit, von der jene Fussgänger behaupten und die Leute in den Autos auch, ja sie ganz besonders, dass sie so vergangen ist, ... als ob sie nie vorhanden gewesen wäre."(38) The question of guilt by passive acquiescence is also touched. The de-

---

(34) Wolfgang Weyrauch, p. 22.
(35) Wolfgang Weyrauch, p. 24.
(36) In Peter Weiss, *Dramen 2,* p. 71.
 ("Sie töteten nicht aus Hass, nicht aus Ueberzeugung, sie töteten nur, weil sie mussten und dies war nicht der Rede wert.")
(37) Wolfgang Weyrauch, p. 24f.
(38) Wolfgang Weyrauch, p. 21.

ranged woman accosts passersby in the street and asks them what they had been thinking when they saw the first yellow star during the NS era. Some people give answers full of compassion, some with anti-Semitic outbursts. Others do not answer at all: "Bei ihnen versagte meine Probe. Sie entzogen sich ihr. Warum? Weil sie unschuldig waren? ... Aber waren sie unschuldig, wenn sie sich nicht darum kümmerten ... Vielleicht fiel ich ihnen auch zur Last. Weshalb? Weil sie ein schlechtes Gewissen hatten, ohne unmittelbar beteiligt zu sein?"(39) The woman attempts to end her suffering by going literally with the *Kopf durch die Wand.(40)* But persecution, condensed in her deranged vision into a visible arrow destined for her destruction follows her, or rather drives her, into complete insanity.

The technique of voicing social or political criticism literarily through the ramblings of a mad person has been used as early as 1834 by Nicolai Gogol in *Diary of a Madman*. Weyrauch has successfully applied this technique to voice his own concern with the postwar German attitude vis-à-vis the Holocaust as he sees it. Through the eyes of the mad woman he magnifies and distorts the still existing anti-Semitic tendencies. The reader might accept the contents of the story as the ramblings of a paranoid. But the grain of truth contained in the distortions might emerge and force him to re-examine his own attitudes. Which of the three answers would he have given?

Intense preoccupation with the Holocaust and post-Holocaust eras is found in the works of Jakov Lind. Lind, now living and working in London, had been forced to leave his native Austria as a child. In spite of having grown up in exile, his working language remained German and he is noted as a member of the German postwar literary gen-

---
(39) Wolfgang Weyrauch, p. 27.
(40) Wolfgang Weyrauch, p. 31.

eration. His prose approximates the style of black comedy, "die mit dem Schrecklichen operiert, als gehöre es zu uns wie etwas Selbstverständliches."(41) As he is a native Viennese, he has focused his attention frequently on the apparent dichotomy of the proverbially charming Viennese and their cruel behavior toward the Jews during the NS period. His writings aim to prove that there was no dichotomy, that the Austrian anti-Semitism was so strongly ingrained that it needed only the official license of the NS regime to become openly rampant. In the title story of his collection *Eine Seele aus Holz,(42)* the main character, a Viennese *Hausbesorger* (Janitor), becomes involved in an altercation with a policeman in a park. As he quarrels with the policeman, bystanders gather around. Not knowing who or what is involved, their immediate reaction is nevertheless:

> Erschiesst's gleich die Judensau. Der Park hat Euch lang genug gehört .... Sittlichkeitsverbrecher! Judengfriess! Meuchelmörder! Hundsfott, jüdischer!(43)

This license to open Jewish persecution granted by the *Saupreussen* (the Austrian name for the Germans) did not diminish the traditional Austrian disdain for them, as the following quotation illustrates: "Was heisst Heil Hitler?" fuhr ihn der Gendarm an. Bei uns heisst das noch immer Heil Oesterreich, Sie Scheisshaufen."(44)

---

(41) Martin Gregor Dellin, "Jakov Lind," in Hermann Kunisch, *Handbuch der deutschen Gegenwartsliteratur* (München: Nymphenburger Verlagshandlung, 1963), pp. 34-35.
(42) Jakov Lind, *Eine Seele aus Holz* (Berlin-Spandau: Hermann Luchterhand Verlag, 1962), pp. 7-126.
(43) Jakov Lind, p. 59.
(44) Jakov Lind, p. 24.

The short story dealing specifically with the postwar era is entitled *Der fromme Bruder.(45)* It takes place in postwar Viennese high society. Its fake gentility, its opportunistic fawning on the conquerors while at the same time despising them, and its unredeemed anti-Semitism are the background before which the macabre farce takes place. Franz, "der Jesuit und Maler, dem man die Klugheit am Gesicht ablesen konnte ... "(46) is a guest at a ball given by the Fürstin Ernestine von Trautenstein to celebrate the end of the Russian occupation: "Bälle gab es oft bei der Fürstin, denn der Trautenstein-Palast war dazu wie geschaffen und der Eintritt, fünf Schilling, half dem fürstlichen Budget ... Die Sandwichs bereitete der Fürst .... höchstpersönlich ... er hielt dabei den Hut auf, die Mayonnaise wischte er sich am Lodenmantel ab, den er über dem Frack trug."(47) Franz had not always been a Jesuit. Both the name and the cloth had been acquired at the end of the war. His real name was Werner Bräutiger and he had been an SS-*Scharführer* in an extermination camp. Like Heinrich Böll's Filskeit in *Wo warst Du Adam,* he too is tortured by a love-hate ambiguity towards the Judeo-Christian ethic. But unlike Filskeit, whose diseased mind was reflected by Böll in a stereotyped manic appearance, Franz is a multifaceted personality. A brilliant painter, conversationalist, and drawingroom habitué, he is in absolute control of himself. Only through his inner monologues is the reader aware of his perversions, which become obvious in the ghastly denouement. While carrying on a sophisticated flirtation with an English music student, for instance, his mind dwells on the following: "Die Erinnerung an das Grandiose der grossen Zeit, als man über Leben und Tod anderer, vor allem Frauen, verfügen konnte ... versetzte Franz in einen hypnotischen Zustand ... nackte Jüdinnen im Aufzug zur End-

---

(45) Jakov Lind, pp. 139-162.
(46) Jakov Lind, p. 139.
(47) Jakov Lind, p. 139.

station deutscher Ehre. Dann platzt die Gnade, sie heisst Cyklon B - wie Barmherzigkeit ... grotesk, obszön, grausam, herrlich, wie ein Hieronymus Bosch ...."(48) Franz is a sadist and a masochist. A Jewess whom he had told after the war that he had been a KZ official had slapped him soundly in answer to the revelation: "Franz dachte an die Jüdin ... die ihm, anstatt in Auschwitz zu sterben, die herrlichste Ohrfeige seines Lebens gegeben hatte. Mit jeder Ohrfeige hatte ... er sich zugeflüstert 'Sie verzeiht! ... Mit Liebe gezüchtigt, oh vergangener Traum der Kindheit!' "(49) Part of Franz's anti-Semitism is based on envy because "...uns Christen hat Gott keine Seele geschenkt. Wir können nur töten, nicht leiden.... Er hasste und verachtete die Stumpfheit seiner christlichen Umwelt ... nur Jüdinnen haben Seele."(50)

The combination of sadism and masochism, pleasure in inflicting pain and death, and desire to experience suffering, lead to his macabre suicide. He is found with his throat cut wearing a black beard and a black wig in imitation of the photograph of one of his Jewish victims. The gruesome imitation is underscored by the addition of a frayed, blood spattered Jewish prayer shawl wrapped around the body. With this black tragic-comedy Lind may have touched on one of the hidden springs of anti-Semitism as he sees it: the desire to kill what one cannot have. If Christians do not have a soul, then they must kill the Jews who have it. The title of the story itself implies the irony to come. *Ein frommer Bruder* in the Viennese idiom is a derogatory term for a sanctimonious hypocrite. Franz fits this description. His absurd death is a fitting end to a cruelly absurd life. Franz is portrayed as neither the stereotype of the cruel SS-man, nor that of the *kleiner Beamter* à la Eichmann. He is a complex

---
(48) Jakov Lind, p. 146.
(49) Jakov Lind, p. 148.
(50) Jakov Lind, p. 148.

individual whose mental aberrations were stronger than his many talents. The secondary characters in the story are distorted caricatures of the postwar Viennese milieu who serve to emphasize the irrationality of the period. Lind presents the portrait of a psychotic killer who had been given official license to satisfy his instincts. When this license is revoked, he cannot operate any more without violating the existing laws. Since he is a great respecter of the laws, he can only murder himself. Like Wolfdietrich Schnurre, Lind also no longer uses any kind of stereotyping. But unlike Schnurre, who lets the realistic situations carry the impact of his work, Lind utilizes caricature and stylizing of his characters and situations to create the gruesome comedy prevalent throughout his work.

The best known play dealing with the post-war attitude of Holocaust perpetrators during the economic reconstruction period is Martin Walser's *Der schwarze Schwan.(51)* This play reveals two states of mind of past perpetrators obviously both suspect to the author: the criminal who has been imprisoned, feels his debt to "society" is paid, and who now enjoys the fruits of his profession as he profited from them in the KZ, and the criminal with a conscience who acknowledges his guilt, but who pleads for understanding of the then existing situation and his predicament. The author has drawn the main characters, two former KZ physicians, with just enough subtle distortions to show his sarcastic opinion of them. Even their names have satirical implications: Libéré, formerly Leibniz, and Goothein. Leibniz, like his great namesake, had deluded himself into believing that he lived in the "best of all possible worlds" when he was committing atrocities in the concentration camps. Now he has become Liberé, the one freed from all delusion. Or perhaps it is the burning

---

(51) Martin Walser, *Der schwarze Schwan* (Frankfurt am Main: Suhrkamp, 1964).

desire to be liberated, freed from his guilt, that has prompted him to live ascetically in self-imposed exile. Goothein, his colleague, also has a name heavy with symbolism. Goothein is a low-German form of *Gut Hein*. *Hein* is the dialect name for the personification of death. Therefore the combination of *good* and *death* implies the jovial killer, the one that went home after a day's work at the crematorium, played with the children in the garden and drank his beer. As if these two sarcastic names were not enough, Walser has also implied heavy irony in the title of the play. *Der schwarze Schwan*(52) was the name given to little Rudi Goothein when he asked an SS-man what the abbreviation *SS* stood for. To use the image of something beautiful like the black swan as the name for something as evil as the SS satirizes the euphemistic Third Reich jargon that called incarceration without recourse *Schutzhaft* (protective custody) and extermination *Endlösung*.

The play hinges on the discovery of his father's past by Goothein's son and namesake, Rudi. He has found an official letter signed with the name *Rudolf Goothein* pertaining to gassing and cremation of prisoners. Rudi Goothein, like Shakespeare's Hamlet, feigns insanity to force the father to a disclosure of his guilt. He even goes as far as Hamlet to stage a play within a play to "catch the conscience of the king."(53) But unlike Hamlet, Rudi's aim is not revenge but destruction of the seed of evil, himself. Since he cannot force his father or Liberé, even through the openly accusing playlet, to confess to their sins, he attempts at least to persuade Liberé's daughter Irm, formerly Hedi, to join him in death. She too as a

---

(52) Martin Walser, p. 41.
(53) William Shakespeare, "Hamlet," in *Shakespeare Complete Works*, Ed. G. B. Garrison (New York: Harcourt, Brace & Co., 1948), Act II, sc. ii, p. 905.

child had been an unwitting witness to her father's crime, and therefore she too should eliminate herself as a carrier of the evil. Irm refuses to join him in death. Here Walser has added an interesting plot complication. Rudi, the son of the man whose conscience is totally untroubled by his crimes, feels the burden, as does Irm's father, Dr. Liberé. Irm, however, unlike her father, is intent on burying the past. Therein she resembles Dr. Goothein: "Günter Blöcker says of the play that Walser aims to show: ... dass man die Schuldigen von damals ohne Berücksichtigung der historischen Provokationen, denen sie ausgesetzt waren, so wenig beurteilen kann, wie die Unschuldigen von heute, denen solche Provokationen erspart blieben."(54) The key sentence for this conclusion is: "Wer nicht hier war zu der Zeit, weiss nicht wozu er im Stand gewesen wäre."(55) But going farther into the play, it becomes apparent that it is only Liberé, the man of sensitivity and strong guilt feelings, who voices these sentiments: "Rudi ... Du hast nie was getan, das weisst Du. Aber hast Du Dir einmal überlegt, was Du getan hättest, wenn es an Dir gewesen wäre ... Trampelst auf jedem herum ... der mit hineingerissen wurde, der Gelegenheit hatte, seine entsetzlichsten Eigenschaften kennenzulernen ... Man muss Gelegenheit haben, vorher kennt man sich nicht."(56) Walser in letting only Liberé voice such thoughts, seems to imply that only such men, being brutally honest with themselves, would plead for understanding of the baseness of their actions. Men like Liberé knew the wrong of their deeds. He seems to try to rationalize his actions with the apparent normalcy of those times: " ... Die elende Glätte, mit der das vor sich ging. Das waren doch ganz normale Tage. Nur dass man das Gefühl hatte, etwas Schlechtes gegessen

---

(54) Günter Blöcker, "Der Realismus X," in *Merkur* XIX 4, 1965, 389-392.
(55) Martin Walser, p. 20.
(56) Martin Walser, p. 51.

zu haben. Eine besondere Uebelkeit andauernd."(57) Again, it is only Liberé who experienced this nausea. Gothein, the jovial killer type, would never utter such words. He did the job expected of him under the existing circumstances. The circumstances changed and " ... ein paar Jahre im Zuchthaus" gave him " ... die Quittung."(58) This satisfying catharsis is reminiscent of the previously mentioned passage in Grass's *Blechtrommel(59)* dealing with a similar type of absolution for all past crimes. Dr. Goothein feels that his debt is marked "paid," and he enjoys his *Wirtschaftswunder* prosperity with a clear conscience.

From the characterization of these two personnages it is apparent that Walser did not plead for general understanding for actions done under *force majeur*. He only points out the rarity of the type that is aware of the nefariousness of his actions and who fears sincerely that the baseness inherent in humanity might become apparent again under similar circumstances.

With this play Walser has added another dimension to his malaise about the middle class German attitudes in the era of the *Wirtschaftswunder:* the general amnesia about the immediate past and its effect on the next generation who demands that an honest accounting be incorporated into a viable future.

---
(57) Martin Walser, p. 50.
(58) Martin Walser, p. 51.
(59) Günter Grass, *Die Blechtrommel*, Chapt. II, see Ftnt. 14.

CONCLUSION

It becomes apparent in the chronological progression that German literature dealing with the Holocaust, pre-Holocaust, and postwar era has shown increasing maturity. From Anna Seghers' nostalgic apologia of an entire upright nation that was suppressed by the evil minority, *Das siebte Kreuz,* to Walser's *Der schwarze Schwan,* German literature has passed through several phases. Regarding this particular topic. Hans Werner Richter's *Sie fielen aus Gottes Hand* and Böll's *Wo warst Du Adam* still evince the strongly philosemitic stereotypes of the immediate postwar era. The Jews were always noble, always good, always victimized. Hannah Arendt's report on the Eichmann trial was the turning point in this type of portrayal. Her definition "the banality of evil" destroyed the daemonic image of the Nazi. It also brought in its suite the long-avoided question of guilt by omission of the passive followers of the Regime and the guilt of the whole world through apathy. Evasive stereotyping, which had allowed the audience to dissociate itself from such German types as were described in the works, gave way to the caricature and stylizing of the average German citizen, successful in the era of the economic miracle through the same virtues that made him successful as an official in the extermination camp. This technique has a didactic purpose by forcing the audience to recognize itself.

The image of the victim changed as well in this period. From the superhumanly good suffering Slomo of Richter's work to the man Moses Matthäus in Walter Jens's *Der Blinde* or Wolfdietrich Schnurre's *Adam,* the accent has shifted from the "poor Jewish victim" to the human being who happened to be Jewish and therefore persecuted. He is now a multifaceted type instead of the stereo-

type. In one extreme case, Rolf Schneider's *Geschichte vom Moischele,* a writer has even slipped into the ugly Jewish stereotype of the Hitler era to prove his objectivity in creating human beings instead of types.

The era of the Holocaust has been treated extensively in German literature with two exceptions: the novel of the day-to-day existence in camp, as Borowski describes it in *This Way for the Gas, Ladies and Gentlemen,* and the novel of Theresienstadt, the concentration camp with the false front. It is not clear why two such literarily fertile topics have not been more closely examined by German writers of the postwar era.

Since the topic is still of relative historical immediacy I would like to consider this study a beginning chapter of a continuous research into the development of German literary attitudes toward the Holocaust. Further inquiry will be necessary and may prove fruitful and enlightening.

LIST OF WORKS CONSULTED

Primary Sources:

Améry, Jean. *Jenseits von Schuld und Sühne.* München: Szczesny Verlag, 1966.

Andersch, Alfred. *Sansibar oder der letzte Grund.* Olten und Freiburg im Breisgau: Walter Verlag, 1957.

Apitz, Bruno. *Nackt unter Wölfen.* Halle a/S: Mitteldeutscher Verlag, 1961.

Böll, Heinrich. *Wo warst Du Adam?* Stuttgart: Henry Goverts Verlag, 1962.

Bor, Josef. *Theresienstätter Requiem.* Trans. Elizabeth Borchardt. Leitersloh: Siegbert Mohn Verlag, 1966.

Borowski, Tadeusz. *This Way for the Gas, Ladies and Gentlemen.* Trans. Barbara Vedder. New York: Viking Press, 1967.

Brecht, Bertolt. *Prosa II.* Frankfurt a/M: Suhrkamp Verlag, 1965.

Donat, Alexander. "Jewish Resistance" *Out of the Whirlwind, a Reader of Holocaust Literature.* Ed. Albert H. Friedländer. Garden City, N.Y.: Doubleday & Co., 1968.

Goes, Albrecht. *Das Brandopfer.* Frankfurt a/M: S. Fischer Verlag, 1954.

Grass, Günter. *Die Blechtrommel.* Berlin-Spandau: Hermann Luchterhand Verlag, 1959.

Hochhuth, Rolf. *Der Stellvertreter.* Reinbek bei Hamburg: Rowohlt Verlag, 1963.

Hoess, Rudolf. *Commandant of Auschwitz*. Trans. C. Fitz Gibbon. London: Weidenfeld & Nicolson, 1959.

Jens, Walter. *Der Blinde*. München: R. Piper & Co., 1964.

Kaiser, Georg. "Von Morgens bis Mitternacht," Stück in zwei Teilen, *Georg Kaiser: Werke*. Ed. Walter Huder. Berlin: Propyläen Verlag, 1970, Vol. I.

Ka-Tzetnick 135 633. *House of Dolls*. London: Frederick Muller Ltd., 1957.

Kipphardt, Heino. *Joel Brand, Die Geschichte eines Geschäfts*. Frankfurt a/M: Suhrkamp Verlag, 1964.

Kluge, Alexander. *Lebensläufe*. Stuttgart: Henry Goverts Verlag, 1962.

Langhoff, Wolfgang. *Die Moorsoldaten; 13 Monate konzentrationslager. Unpolitischer tatsachenbericht*. Zürich: Schweizer Spiegel, 1935.

Lind, Jakov. *Eine Seele aus Holz*. Berlin-Spandau: Hermann Luchterhand Verlag, 1962.

Lustig, Arnost. *Diamonds in the Night*. Trans. George Theiner. London: Hutchinson of London, 1962.

Lustig, Arnost. *Night and Hope*. Trans. Iris Urwin. Prague: Artia, 1962.

Marcuse, Ludwig. *Mein Zwanzigstes Jahrhundert*. Frankfurt a/M: Fischer Bücherei, 1968.

Moosdorf, Johanna. *Nebenan*. Frankfurt a/M: Suhrkamp Verlag, 1961.

Remarque, Erich Maria. *Arc de Triomphe*. Zürich, 1946.

_____ *Der Funke Leben*. Köln-Berlin: Kiepenheuer & Witsch, 1952.

_____ *Im Westen nichts Neues*. Köln-Berlin: Kiepenheuer & Witsch, 1962.

Richter, Hans Werner. *Sie fielen aus Gottes Hand*. München: Verlag Kurt Desch, 1951.

Sachs, Nelly. "Eli, Ein Mysterienspiel vom Leider Israel" in *Nelly Sachs. Das Leiden Israel*. Frankfurt a/M: Suhrkamp Verlag, 1965.

Schallück, Paul. *Engelbert Reinecke*. Frankfurt a/M: Fischer Verlag, 1961.

Schneider, Rolf. "Die Geschichte vom Moischele" in *Rolf Schneider*. Stücke. Berlin: Henschelverlag, Kunst und Gesellschaft, 1970.

_____ "prozess in nürnberg" in *Rolf Schneider Stücke*. Berlin: Henschelverlag, Kunst und Gesellschaft, 1970.

Schnurre, Wolfdietrich. *Eine Rechnung, die nicht aufgeht*. München: List Verlag, 1964.

_____ *Man sollte dagegen sein*. Olten und Freiburg im Breisgau: Walter Verlag, 1960.

Shakespeare, William. "Hamlet" in *Shakespeare Complete Works*. Ed. G.B. Garrison. New York: Harcourt, Brace & Co., 1948.

Seghers, Anna. *Das siebte Kreuz*. Amsterdam: Querido Verlag, N.V.

_____ *Der Ausflug der toten Mädchen*. New York: Aurora Verlag, 1946.

Semprun, Jorge. *The Long Voyage*. Trans. Richard Seaver. New York: Grove Press, 1964.

Walser, Martin. *Der schwarze Schwan*. Frankfurt a/M: Suhrkamp Verlag, 1964.

_____ *Halbzeit*. Frankfurt a/M: Suhrkamp Verlag, 1960.

Weiss, Peter. "Die Ermittlung" in *Peter Weiss. Dramen 2*. Frankfurt a/M: Suhrkamp Verlag, 1968.

Weiss, Peter. "Meine Ortschaft" in *Peter Weiss, Rapporte*. Frankfurt a/M: Suhrkamp Verlag, 1968.

Werner, Bruno. *Die Galeere*. Frankfurt a/M: G. B. Fischer Verlag, 1958.

Weyrauch, Wolfgang. *Mein Schiff, das heisst Taifun*. Olten und Freiburg im Breisgau: Walter Verlag, 1959.

Wiechert, Ernst. *Der Totenwald*. Zürich: Rascher Verlag, 1946.

Wiesel, Elie. *Night*. Trans. Stella Ridway. New York: Hill & Wang, 1960.

Zweig, Stefan. *Schachnovelle*. Frankfurt a/M: Fischer Verlag, 1957.

Secondary Sources:

Alvarez, A. "The literature of the Holocaust." *Commentary*, 37, Nov., 1964, pp. 65-69.

Blöcker, Günter. "Der Realismus X." *Merkur*, XIX, 4, 1965, pp. 389-392.

Carmichael, Joel. "Peter Weiss' Auschwitz." *Encounter*, XXVI, 1, Jan. 1966, pp. 90-93.

Davidowicz, Lucy S. "Toward a History of the Holocaust in Memory of Max Weinreich." *Commentary*, 52, Apr. 1969, pp. 51-56.

Dellin, Martin Gregor. "Jakov Lind." *Handbuch der deutschen Gegenwartsliteratur*. Ed. Hermann Kunisch, München: Nymphenburger Verlagshandlung, 1963, pp. 34-35.

Domin, Hilde. "Offener Brief an Nelly Sachs." *Nelly Sachs zu Ehren*. Ed. Walter A. Berendson. Frankfurt a/M: Suhrkamp Verlag, 1960, p. 194 f.

Elster, Hansjörg. "Erich Maria Remarque." *Handbuch der deutschen Gegenwartsliteratur.* Ed. Hermann Kunisch. München: Nymphenburger Verlagshandlung, 1963, p. 124.

Frisch, Max. "Stimmen eines anderen Deutschlands." *Neue Schweizer Rundschau,* XIII, 1945-46, pp. 537-547.

Gray, Simon, "A Man of Style." *The New Statesman,* LXXIII, 622, May 5, 1967.

Halprin, Milton. *Messengers from the Dead.* Philadelphia: Westminster Press, 1970, p. 111.

Kazin, Alfred. "The Vicar of Christ." *The storm over The deputy.* Ed. E. Bentley. New York: Grove Press, 1965, p. 104.

Kipphardt, Heino. "Anmerkungen zu Joel Brand." *Heino Kipphardt: Joel Brand, Die Geschichte eines Geschäfts.* Frankfurt a/M: Suhrkamp Verlag, 1964, p. 141 141.

Korman, Gert *The Holocaust in American Historiography,* paper read at the Eigthy-Sixth Annual Meeting of the American Historical Association held in New York on Dec. 28-30, 1971.

Langenbucher, Wolfgang. "Unterhaltung als Märchen und als Politik." *Tendenzen der Deutschen Literatur seit 1945.* Ed. Thomas Koebner. Stuttgart: Alfred Kröner Verlag, 1971, p. 326.

Levy, Günther, Pius XII, the Jews and the German Catholic Church." *The storm over The deputy.* Ed. Eric Bentley. New York: Grove Press, 1964, p. 202.

Lexikon deutschsprachiger Schriftsteller. Ed. Günter Albrecht. Leipzig: Bibliografisches Institut VEB, 1967, p. 40.

Mayer, Hans. *Zur deutschen Literatur der Zeit: Zusammenhänge, Schriftsteller, Bücher.* Reinbek bei Hamburg: Rowohlt Verlag, 1967.

Melchinger, Siegfried. "Anmerkungen zu den Spielen" *Nelly Sachs zu Ehren*. Ed. Walter A. Berendson. Frankfurt a/M: Suhrkamp Verlag, 1966, p. 162.

Meyer, Michael A. "The Religious Thought of Emil L. Fackenheim; Judaism after Auschwitz" *Commentary*, 53 6, June 1972, p. 55-62.

Morgan, Bayard, Quincy. *Ernst Wiechert, der Mensch und sein Werk*. München, 1951, p. 234.

Poliakov, Leon. "Pope Pius XII and the Nazis." *The storm over The deputy,* Ed. Eric Bentley. New York: Grove Press, 1965, p. 230.

Reich-Ranicki, Marcel. *Deutsche Literatur im West und Ost*. München: Piper Verlag, 1966.

Rilla, Paul. *Die Erzählerin Anna Seghers*. Berlin: Schriftenreihe der deutschen Akademie der Künste, 1950.

Rischbieter, Henning. *Peter Weiss*. Velben: Friedrichs Verlag, 1967.

Rollins, E. Wm. & Zohn, Harry, Ed. *Men of Dialogue: Martin Buber and Albrecht Goes*. New York: Funk and Wagnall, 1969.

Sander, Volkmar. *Die Faszination des Bösen: Zur Wandlung des Menschenbildes*. Göttingen: Sachse und Pohl Verlag, 1968.

Schirokauer, Arno. "Zu Wiechert's Totenwald" *Neue Rundschau,* 1947. Stockholm: Berman Fischer Verlag, 1947, p. 348-52.

Schneider, Rolf. "Gedanken über Theater" *Rolf Schneider: Stücke*. Berlin: Henschelverlag, Kunst und Gesellschaft, 1970.

Seghers, Anna. "Bewahrung und Entdeckung" *Neue Deutsche Literatur,* XI, 8, 1963, p. 55.

Theater heute "Sonderausgabe" Bad Godesberg: Friedrich Verlag, 1965.